ALEXANDER HAMILTON'S GUIDE TO LIFE

ALEXANDRA RIPLEY'S SCARLETT

ALEXANDER
HAMILTON'S
Guide to Life

JEFF WILSER

THREE RIVERS PRESS
NEW YORK

Library of Congress Cataloging-in-Publication Data
Names: Wilser, Jeff, author.
Title: Alexander Hamilton's guide to life / Jeff Wilser.
Description: New York: Three Rivers Press, 2016. | Includes
bibliographical references.
Identifiers: LCCN 2016030203| ISBN 9780451498090 (hc) |
ISBN 9780451498106 (eISBN)
Subjects: LCSH: Hamilton, Alexander, 1757–1804—Ethics. | Hamilton,
Alexander, 1757–1804—Philosophy. | Conduct of life.
Classification: LCC E302.6.H2 W75 2016 | DDC 973.4092—dc23
LC record available at https://lccn.loc.gov/2016030203

ISBN 978-0-451-49809-0
Ebook ISBN 978-0-451-49810-6

Printed in the United States of America

Book design by Andrea Lau
Illustrations by Kent Barton
Cover design by Jake Nicolella
Cover and page xi illustration by Mark Summers
Page 318 photograph by Dirty Sugar Photography

5 7 9 10 8 6

First Edition

To everyone really into Hamilton . . .
and to those not yet really into Hamilton.

CONTENTS

—

10. HONOR

" 'Tis my maxim to let the plain naked truth speak for itself;
and if men won't listen to it, 'tis their own fault."

—ALEXANDER HAMILTON

INTRODUCTION

—

ALEXANDER HAMILTON WAS A FOUNDING FATHER, a war hero, the creator of the modern economy, and the winner of a silver medal for "2nd place in Dueling." But let's not kid ourselves. Until recently, people only knew three things about Hamilton: that he's on the $10 bill, that he lived a really long time ago, and that he (probably) wasn't a President.

So why the renewed interest?

On the most obvious level, of course, Hamilton fever is owed to the triumph of Lin-Manuel Miranda's musical. It connects the old and the young, the Left and the Right, the insiders and the outsiders. "It's brilliant," gushed theater critic Barack Obama. "This is the only thing that Dick Cheney and I have agreed on in my entire political career." It will be sold out through 2047. Credit the genius of Miranda, credit the soundtrack, and credit the electric (and thrillingly diverse) cast.

Yet there's a deeper reason we're drawn to Hamilton—and that's the man himself. He feels somehow *different* from the other Founders, who, with their wise words and their marble statues, can seem more like myths than men.

Hamilton strikes us as human. Flawed. Fearless. Reckless.

He was an underdog. He dared to champion the unpopular. And like so many of us, he began at the bottom and clawed his way up. Whereas the other Founders were born with money and connections—and, in many cases, slave plantations—Hamilton was an orphan who sailed to America on a boat, armed only with big plans and bigger dreams.

He took classes at night, taught himself Latin, jumped at every chance for self-improvement. As a teenager, when stuck in a ho-hum job at a trading shop, he used the gig to learn bookkeeping, memorize foreign currencies, and master the art of negotiation. This lesson is timeless. For those of us not born into royalty, it can be reassuring—even inspiring—to know you can do so much with so little.

Hamilton's life is jam-packed with lessons; anyone can learn from his core principles. True, it's unlikely that you will ever fire a musket at the British, but we can all learn from the way that he led his troops, organized his time, and viewed the world through a wider lens. Anyone with a job—at any age, in any field—can appreciate the way he found a worthy mentor (George Washington), spoke with authority (even when he had none), and hustled for a promotion. And anyone who wants to win a duel, well, should maybe go purchase *Aaron Burr's Guide to Life*.

Hamilton didn't have much money, but he made up for it with a swagger, intellectual curiosity, clear vision, and a bottomless appetite for work. "Alexander Hamilton did what we do; he just did it earlier. Because he was a great man, he generally did it better," suggests biographer Richard Brookhiser. "His life, and the lives of his peers, can guide and caution us."

That is the goal of this book. It is not a traditional biography. Instead, it's the kind of manual that Hamilton would have written himself, perhaps, had he lived to be an old man. That's a bold claim, and of course Hamilton's actual *Guide to Life* would have been smarter, deeper, longer, and Founding Fatherier.

Yet we do know this: Hamilton loved his "maxims." In one collection of his writings, he used the word 209 times. (That's not a joke. I counted.) He clearly put real thought into his personal code of conduct.

On how to speak: " 'Tis my maxim to let the naked truth speak for itself, and if men won't listen to it, 'tis their own fault; they must be contented to suffer for it."

On enjoying the moment: "It is a maxim of my life to enjoy the present good with the highest relish, and to soften the present evil by a hope of future good."

On the merits of aggressiveness: "I hold it an established maxim, that there is three to one in favor of the party attacking."

So, in some ways, this is a very modern kind of history book. It scrambles a mix of history, life advice, and the occasional reference to Luke Skywalker. Yet the format is ancient. And it's a format that's inspired by Hamilton's own writings. As a soldier, young Captain Hamilton scribbled into his army journal, jotting down facts and lessons that he found interesting. He took many notes on Plutarch, who had a novel way of telling history: the ancient Greek shared the stories and struggles of great men (alas, always men, never women), and then he sussed out the implied life lessons. "The virtues of these great men," writes Plutarch, "serve me as a sort of looking glass, in which I may see how to adjust and adorn my own life." Hamilton devoured Plutarch's *Lives*. It's only fitting that we give him the same treatment.

But how do we know Hamilton's life lessons? Fair question. For guidance I leaned heavily on the towering works of Ron Chernow, Richard Brookhiser, Michael E. Newton, James Flexner, and a small library of historians. (These heroes have built a mountain with their research. We can now climb that mountain and admire the view, contemplate it, learn from it.) I trekked to the West Indies to trace Hamilton's footsteps on Nevis and St. Croix, I interviewed scholars, I rummaged through Hamilton's old letters and manifestos, and I spoke with the next best thing to a living Alexander Hamilton—Douglas Hamilton, his fifth great-grandson, who often thinks about the advice from his ancestor. "I was actually planning on writing a book like this," Hamilton tells me, laughing a bit. "Now I don't have to. Thanks for checking off that box for me."

This book is not the exhaustive, comprehensive, list-every-fact book on Hamilton. Those books have been written and they are excellent. This is a different beast. It's intended to inspire. Add perspective. Hopefully amuse.

It's organized by topic, from Self-Improvement to Honor, with a few stops in Money, Romance, and Leadership along the way. Theoretically you could skip around and read it out of order, but don't. Hamilton's rags-to-riches (-to-debt) story is just too good *not* to tell—even if you've heard it before—so the book, while not strictly linear, sprints through the arc of his life. To paraphrase Robert Caro, we'll follow Hamilton's rise to power, use of power, and fall from power.

Who should read this book?

Anyone obsessed with the musical: This will help you go deeper, appreciate more of the historical context, parse the fact from the fiction, and realize that Miranda is even more of a genius than you thought.

History buffs: "I've read sixty-three books on Hamilton," the founder of the Alexander Hamilton Awareness Society, Rand Scholet, tells me. This book is also for folks like Rand. It's a fresh take that will add perspective, uncover new gems, and for those who truly know their Hamilton, draw some knowing smiles.

Those new to Hamilton: No prior knowledge is required. Buckle up.

Everyone, actually: The guide offers nuggets of wisdom that are both useful and uplifting. Hamilton's maxims can change how we think about our jobs, what we value in life, and how we treat our friends and family. The book will also explore *why* Hamilton was so crucial to the founding of America.

This is not a "How To" book that will give you Hamilton's shredded abs. And it won't tell you how to get rich quick. Yet it cracks open his playbook, suggesting insight into how he went from abandoned son to Founding Father. Some lessons are literal and can be applied directly to your life. Others show us, through Hamilton's actions, how to be more successful. And because Hamilton was a red-blooded man who made mistakes, still others guide us on what *not* to do. Some lessons are subtle, some are provocative, and some are a bit of a joke. (You'll know which is which.)

The book makes no claims of objectivity. It is, without a doubt, the second-most-pro-Hamilton book in history. (The first? *The Papers of Alexander Hamilton,* written by Alexander Hamilton. It comes in 27 volumes.)

Yet it won't flinch from his faults. He was a man, not a saint. We tend to think of the Founding Fathers as old guys with powdered wigs saying high-minded things about government. But they were ordinary (if gifted) people who were driven by ambition and frustrated by their jobs; who liked to have a laugh (and maybe a mistress) along the way; who fell in love, feared for their children, worried about death. The human condition hasn't changed. Their guide can be our guide.

Hamilton was guided, more than anything else, by one foundational concept: an unbending sense of honor. This is what makes him a tragic hero. It's what made him tick, it's what forged modern America, and it's also what got him killed.

1
SELF-IMPROVEMENT

SPEAK WITH AUTHORITY . . . EVEN IF YOU HAVE NONE

RISE ABOVE YOUR STATION

—

"[I] would willingly risk my life
tho' not my Character to exalt my Station."

HAMILTON'S EARLY YEARS ARE MURKY. Historians debate the details. Yet there can be no doubt that he's the only Founding Father whose mother, Rachael Fawcett, was accused in court of "whoring with everyone."

This wasn't a happy home. This wasn't a happy place. On the Caribbean island of St. Croix, several years before Hamilton's birth, Rachael was "twice guilty of adultery," according to her first husband, which, in those enlightened times, gave him the legal right to toss her into prison. So he locked her in a dungeon. (I've been inside the prison cell. It's dark, hot, and has a tiny window that looks out on the clear blue sea, almost as a taunt.)

With Rachael behind bars, her husband hoped that "everything would change to the better and that she, as a wedded wife, would change her unholy way of life and live with him." Ah, true love! He let her out of jail. Somehow the plan backfired, the dungeon failed to melt her heart, and Rachael fled and didn't look back.

She took a ferry to an even smaller island, St. Kitts, that throbbed with the sugar and slave trades. She met a Scot named

James Hamilton. On an even *smaller* island, Nevis, Rachael gave birth to two boys, one named Alexander. She was still married to the dungeon-master of a first husband, however, which meant that Alexander Hamilton, technically, was born a bastard. The first husband eventually filed for a separation; the divorce papers called her "shameless, rude and ungodly" and the mother of "whorechildren."

The family soon moved back to St. Croix. The island was brutal. Alexander, or Alex, as he was called as a toddler, grew up in a land that had 90 percent of its population chained in slavery. The slaves made the sugar. "The whites lived in fear of slave rebellions. By law, every white man had to be armed with a gun, sixteen cartridges with balls, and a sword or cutlass," explains biographer James Flexner. "To keep terror perpetually alive among the blacks, it was legislated that if a slave struck a white man, he would lose the hand he struck it with. If he drew blood, he could be executed."

Then things took a turn for the worse.

Alex's father went bankrupt and left home. (Historians still aren't sure why.) Then the family got sick. Rachael caught tropical fever, confining her to a bed that would drip with blood, sweat, and vomit. The house had only one bed, which meant that Alex either slept next to his coughing mother or he slept on the floor. The doctors treated Rachael with "bloodletting" and "alcohol for her head." He was eleven when she died. The probate court ruled that Alex would get nothing from her modest estate, as he and his brother were "obscene children."

Then things took a turn for the worse.

Alex's cousin volunteered to look after the boys, but for reasons still unknown he committed suicide. The legal record states that he "stabbed or shot himself to death." His grandmother died. His uncle died. His aunt died.

Yet Alex refused to think like a victim. When he was just twelve years old, he wrote to his friend Edward Stevens (or "Neddy"), declaring:

> *My Ambition is [so] prevalent that I contemn the grov'ling and condition of a Clerk . . . to which my Fortune condemns me and would willingly risk my life tho' not my Character to exalt my Station.*

He ends the letter on one of history's great non sequiturs: "I shall conclude saying I wish there was a war."

It's Hamilton's oldest surviving letter. Even as a child he burned with a desire to do whatever it takes—work harder, get smarter, prove valor on a battlefield—to improve himself . . . so long as it did not compromise his honor.

There's one more lesson here. The letter contains another, trickier, more archaic passage that isn't quoted as often:

> *I'm confident, Ned that my youth excludes me from any hopes of immediate preferment nor do I desire it, but I mean to prepare the way for futurity . . . My folly makes me ashamed and [I] beg you'll conceal it, yet Neddy we have seen such schemes successful when the <u>Projector</u> is constant.*

Okay, some real talk: On the first read, that paragraph is nearly incomprehensible. Yet it contains the keys to Hamilton's playbook. Douglas Hamilton (the fifth great-grandson) thinks of this advice all the time, he lives by it, and he shares it with his grandchildren, who are often baffled. "People ask me, *Projector*? What the hell does that even mean?"

Let's look at the sentence again:

> . . . *we have seen such schemes successful when the* <u>*Projector*</u> *is constant* . . .

The Projector is the thing that is projecting an outcome, the thing doing the work. You. If the *projector is constant*—with steady work—then you can prepare yourself for a better future. This is how you rise above your station.

He had no parents, no inheritance, no formal education, and no obvious path to success. Yet he knew it was possible. He believed. From the very beginning, it would always be Alexander Hamilton against the world.

That's a fair fight.

STEAL (NEW SKILLS) FROM EVERY JOB

—

"[A childhood job in a trading shop was] the
most useful part of [my] education.'"

THINK BACK TO YOUR first job. Maybe it was delivering pizzas, waiting tables, or sacking groceries. Hamilton had a job like that. When his mom was still alive he helped her run a shop below their home, and then, when still a kid (possibly as young as *eight*), he worked at a trading shop called Beekman and Cruger. It's the kind of job that most kids hate. He must have swept the floors, wiped the counters, and spent hours tediously double-checking the inventory.

Yet the job offered something more. For perhaps the first time in his life, Hamilton began to glimpse a larger world. Some quick context: When people say that Hamilton was from "a forgotten spot" or "the middle of nowhere," that's not entirely true. Every morning, as a fleet of ships hugged the wharfs of St. Croix, he woke up to a bustling commercial hub. Sugar was to the Caribbean what oil now is to the Middle East. The "white gold" could make or break empires. (How valuable was the Caribbean? In the treaty of 1763, after a military defeat, France was forced to give Britain either most of Canada or the tiny islands of Martinique,

Guadeloupe, and St. Lucia. They thought about it for maybe five seconds. Then they kissed Canada goodbye.)

Hamilton saw all of the wheeling and dealing. Since the shop traded with all parts of the globe, it forced him to learn about things like foreign exchange rates and currency fluctuations— French livres, German marks, Danish kroner. He learned book-keeping. Inventory control. When cargo sailed to the docks of St. Croix, young Hamilton unloaded the goods and lugged them to a Scale House, where he measured the lumber, pork, fish, rope, cattle, and corn. (The Scale House still exists. And it's only a Frisbee toss away from where his mother was once imprisoned, which means he saw the jail every day.) He did his chores well. So his boss, the Dickensian-named Nicholas Cruger, soon gave him more clout: Alex would decide *where* the cargo should be sold, *when* to sell it, and *how much* it should cost.

"The *when to sell* sounds obvious, but it's not always," explains historian Michael E. Newton. Hamilton once inspected a boatload of scrawny mules. "A worse parcel of mules never was seen," reported Hamilton. The easy move would have been to sell the mules right away and be done with it. Instead he fed them, waited for them to grow healthier, and then sold them at a higher profit.

He learned supply and demand, price elasticity, and the art of negotiation. This gave him an early nose for global finance. (Meanwhile, far away in the thirteen colonies, his eventual rivals would go through puberty learning a much simpler economic model: Watch your slaves pick cotton. Sell. Pour more lemonade.)

As a clerk, Hamilton had to haggle with scoundrels and smugglers, which taught him another life lesson—people cheat—that would, years later, spawn his idea for a fleet of boats that would curb smuggling (the fleet would become the Coast Guard). The job also taught him the need for a solid currency. And he learned that every business needs access to cash, capital, and credit.

The "steal new skills" mentality, of course, doesn't mean that you need to *love* your tedious job. Not even Hamilton pretended to, complaining to Neddy of the "grov'ling . . . condition of a clerk." But flip the mindset. Learn from the job. Exploit it. Fill your bag of skills.

Not even dead-end jobs are a dead end.

WHEN WAS HAMILTON BORN?

Nothing about Alexander Hamilton is ever simple. Not even his birthday. Everyone agrees on the date of January 11, but historians debate the year itself.

For nearly two hundred years, most scholars accepted that Hamilton was born in 1757. One key bit of evidence? Hamilton himself cited 1757 as his birth year. Then, in 1939, a newly discovered document, from a St. Croix probate court, pointed to a birth year of 1755.

Academics and historians have spent years and hundreds of pages digging through the weeds, but basically, it comes down to one of two things. Either:

1) Hamilton lied about his age; or
2) The clerk made a mistake.

The "Hamilton lied" camp suggests that when he enrolled in college, he deliberately shaved two years off his age to appear more like a prodigy. The "clerk erred" camp notes that *on the very same document*, the clerk misspelled the name of Hamilton's mother. As Brookhiser concludes, "Believing that a man is more likely to know his own birthday than a clerk in a probate court, I will accept 1757." Same.

READ WHEN OTHERS PLAY

—

"[Employ] all your leisure in reading."

THE "READING IS FUNDAMENTAL" CAMPAIGN could begin and end with Alexander Hamilton. Books were the fuel that made his engine go. And his love of reading started at a young age. We don't know much about Hamilton's mother, but we do know that she had a library of thirty-four books, a stash that likely included Machiavelli, Plutarch, and Alexander Pope. You know, kids' books.

He ripped through these. He ripped through every library. He devoured classics, novels, poetry, philosophy, history, and fat economic treatises that would make you and me weep. Yet this is what set Hamilton apart: he carved out time to read when others wouldn't.

Years later, as a young man in Washington's army, while burdened by a dawn-to-dusk schedule of artillery and bloodshed, he somehow found the energy to crack open books and improve himself. Who else would spend his downtime reading Malachy Postlethwayt's *Universal Dictionary of Trade and Commerce*? The book was large and heavy and wasn't available on the Kindle.

"The dictionary took the form of two ponderous, folio-sized volumes," notes Ron Chernow, "and it is touching to think of young Hamilton lugging them through the chaos of war."

Instead of playing cards with the other officers, Hamilton would cozy up with this almanac and think about its content, scribbling notes in his journal like, "When you can get more of foreign coin, [the] coin of your native exchange is said to be high and the reverse low."

The reading paid off immediately. Still ensconced in Washington's command center, the young officer wrote a bold letter to a congressman that flashed, for the first time, the glimmer of his financial brilliance. "The present plan is the product of some reading on the subjects of commerce and finance," he wrote with some understatement, and a "want of leisure" prevented him from writing even more. Young Hamilton's "present plan" was a six-thousand-word, twelve-point program that foreshadowed his grand designs as treasury secretary.

You don't have to be a freakishly gifted Founding Father (or Mother) to benefit from this mindset. Some basic math will help us bridge from Hamilton legend to something that's doable: The average reading speed is 250 words per minute. The average page has around 250 words. So if you skip just one TV show and read for just one hour every day, that works out to 420 pages a week, or, on average, 50 books a year. Over, say, 40 years of adulthood, that adds up to a sprawling, floor-to-ceiling library of over 2,000 books. It can be done.

Hamilton knew that books can worm their way into your brain in surprising ways, sparking ideas that power the imagination. The examples are infinite, such as the time in 2008 when, on the way to a vacation in Mexico, an artist picked up a book to read on the beach. Thankfully this artist was Lin-Manuel Miranda, and thankfully the book was Ron Chernow's *Alexander Hamilton*.

SPEAK WITH AUTHORITY...
EVEN IF YOU HAVE NONE

—

"Reflect continually on the unfortunate
voyage you have just made."

HAMILTON'S BOSS AT THE TRADING SHOP, Nicholas
Cruger, soon grew to trust the kid. So when the
boss had to leave the shop for a few months, he put
Hamilton in charge.

At age fourteen, Hamilton immediately acted like he owned
the place. He instructed one captain to "remember you are to
make three trips this season and unless you are very diligent, you
will be too late as our crops will be early." Later, when someone
botched a job, young Hamilton admonished him to "reflect continually on the unfortunate voyage you have just made."

The kid wrote like a seasoned Wall Street trader: "I sold all
your lumber off immediately at 16 pounds. Luckily enough, the
price of that article being now reduced to 12 pounds . . . Your
mahogany is of the very worst kind." No timidity, no indecisive-
ness, no signs of backing down. When a man's mahogany isn't up
to snuff, you call him on it.

While his boss was away, Hamilton even had the audacity to
fire the shop's lawyer, as he was "very negligent . . . and trifled
away a good deal of money."

Years later, in the Revolutionary War, Hamilton's nervy tone would earn the respect of senior officers and politicians. When still a junior secretary, he wrote to a brigadier general that Washington was "so much pestered with matters which cannot be avoided that I am obliged to refrain from troubling him . . . especially as I conceive the only answer he would give may be given by myself." Translation: You will take your orders from me.

At nearly every stage of Hamilton's career, from age eight until the day he died, he would, almost without exception, be the youngest man in the room. He made up for his youth with an assertive voice. You get the sense that when Hamilton came out of the womb, he somehow told his mother, "I am ready for the milk. Please do not be frugal. When I finish, you should prepare yourself for subsequent feedings."

It's human nature. When people speak as if they have power, we assume that they actually do. Whether you're in corporate America, teaching a class of high school students, disciplining your kids, running a shop, or writing to generals in the Revolutionary War, if you talk like the boss, you will soon be the boss.

UNLEASH YOUR HOBBIES

——

"[I have] always had a strong propensity to literary pursuits."

Y OUNG ALEX FOUND TIME for at least one hobby: writing. On this hot and brutal island of sugar and slave trading, Alexander could transport himself, through his paper and quill, to a world of his own imagination. He began writing poetry.

Inspired partially by Alexander Pope, his poems could be philosophical (of course), playful, spiritual, and even erotic. In 1771, someone with the initials A.H.* sent a polite pitch to the *Royal Danish American Gazette*:

> *Sir, I am a youth of about seventeen, and consequently such an attempt as this must be presumptuous; but if, upon your perusal, you think the following piece worthy of a place in your paper, by inserting it you'll much oblige.*
> *—Your obedient servant, A.H.*

---

* The poem's authorship is in dispute. Historians still debate whether this A.H. is actually the A.H. we know and love, but the editors of the National Archives say "it is a reasonable assumption that Hamilton was the author."

The poem from A.H.:

Celia's an artful little slut;
Be fond, she'll kiss, et cetera—but
She must have all her will;
For, do but rub her 'gainst the grain
Behold a storm, blow winds and rain,
Go bid the waves be still.
So, stroking puss's velvet paws
How well the jade conceals her claws
And purrs; but if at last
You hap to squeeze her somewhat hard,
She spits—her back up—prenez garde;
Good faith she has you fast.

"Artful little slut"! That's one ballsy hook. Another, from the same A.H:

In yonder mead my love I found
Beside a murm'ring brook reclin'd:
Her pretty lambkins dancing round
Secure in harmless bliss.
I bad the waters gently glide,
And vainly hush'd the heedless wind,
Then, softly kneeling by her side,
I stole a silent kiss—
She wak'd, and rising sweetly blush'd
By far more artless than the dove:

With eager haste I onward rush'd,
And clasp'd her in my arms;
Encircled thus in fond embrace
Our panting hearts beat mutual love—
A rosy-red o'er spread her face
And brighten'd all her charms.

. . . and so on.

Alex soon caught the eye of a Presbyterian minister, the Reverend Hugh Knox, who had journeyed to the West Indies as an evangelist. Knox was a man of books and culture, and at Princeton he had received his education, in one whopper of a coincidence, from the father of Aaron Burr.

Knox saw something in Hamilton. *Keep writing,* he told the kid. So Hamilton doubled down on his hobby. He practiced. He honed.

Then he unleashed.

On August 31, 1772, when Hamilton was fifteen years old, a hurricane hit St. Croix. It shattered homes and uprooted trees, demolishing the island. So Hamilton wrote about it. Technically, he simply wrote a letter to his father (who by then had left the family), but the work would soon find a much larger audience. The local *Gazette* published Hamilton's letter anonymously.

"It began about dusk, at North, and raged very violently till ten o'clock," begins Hamilton's narrative. He describes:

The roaring of the sea and wind, fiery meteors flying about it in the air, the prodigious galore of almost perpetual lightning, the crash of the falling houses, and the ear-piercing

shrieks of the depressed, were sufficient to strike astonish-
ment into angels.

(Is that you, Herman Melville?)

Foreshadowing his later political analysis, he even has the audacity to pass judgment on the island's governor, noting that he
"had issued several very salutary and humane regulations, and
both in his publick and private measures, has shewn himself *the
Man*." (By the way . . . "Publick"? "Shewn"? If you're curious
about the occasional funky spellings and Capitalizations, see the
endnotes.)

The letter went viral, and Hamilton's identity was soon revealed. As legend has it, the whole island seemed to say, Wait,
hold up, a frickin' *teenager* wrote this? Within weeks, the money-
men of St. Croix took up a collection and raised a scholarship, of
sorts, to send him off to college in mainland America. The kid
had talent. The kid was going places.

None of this would have happened if Hamilton kept his poems
to himself, doodling in his journal, too shy to share. We can learn
from this. Indulge in your hobbies. Get good. Have confidence.
Then unleash your hobbies onto the world.

Just a few weeks later, the teenager took one final walk to the
docks of St. Croix. Carrying little or no luggage, he climbed onto
a boat; the boat eased from the wharf, and perhaps he glanced
back to the trading shop and the slave market and the jail where
his mother had once been imprisoned. The boat sliced through
the water and the island soon became a tiny dot in the distance.
He fixed his gaze north. To New York City.

TURN GRIT INTO GENIUS

—

*"All the genius I have lies in this . . . It is
the fruit of labor and thought."*

AMILTON SAILED TO AMERICA in a blaze of ambition. Literally—the boat was on fire. The ship had somehow caught fire during the three-week journey, putting him in "imminent peril." Buckets of water extinguished the flames, the boat stayed afloat, the immigrant lived.

As soon as he arrived, the fifteen-year-old must have felt at home. With a population of twenty thousand, New York City was energetic, fast-paced, cosmopolitan—and, to some, offputting. (Just like Hamilton.) What was Manhattan like back in 1772? A lot like it is now. John Adams found that New Yorkers "talk very loud, very fast, and all together. If they ask you a question, before you utter three words of your answer, they will break out upon you again and walk away."

Hamilton didn't dawdle. Armed with letters of introduction from Hugh Knox, he soon made connections that helped him attend a prep school at Elizabethtown, New Jersey, where he scrambled to play catch-up. Without much (or any) proper schooling in the Caribbean, he knew he lagged behind his classmates.

So he crammed. He blasted through a decade of schoolwork in less than a year. "During the winter [Hamilton] was accustomed to labor until midnight," explains his son John C. Hamilton. "In summer, it was his habit to retire at dawn to the quiet of a nearby cemetery, where he was often seen preparing his lessons for the day. By these exertions, he made rapid progress."

He rocketed through lessons in Greek, Latin, mathematics, and other guilty pleasures. Then he was ready for college. At first he applied to Princeton, but he had one special request: *Let me do it in less than four years. Ideally, two.* The school gave him an oral examination. He aced it. The president of Princeton, however, said that the request "was contrary to the usage of the College." *Denied.* (Adding insult to injury, in the past, Princeton *had* offered the fast-track program to another promising young teenager, Aaron Burr.)

Fine. If Princeton wouldn't let him run faster, he would find a college that would. He applied to King's College, in Lower Manhattan, which would later rebrand itself as Columbia. Again he requested the fast-track program. This time they accepted.

Let's pause here. The advice of "work really long hours" is not particularly inspiring, yet it's critical to understanding Hamilton. He outhustled everyone. As he explains it:

Men give me credit for some genius. All the genius I have lies in this, when I have a subject in hand I study it profoundly. Day and night it is before me. I explore it in all its bearings. My mind becomes pervaded with it. Then the effort that I have made is what people are pleased to call the fruit of genius. It is the fruit of labor and thought.

This, though, is his real genius: Staying focused on Latin while being distracted by hookers. Literally. King's College—located downtown, on present-day Broadway—was right next to the city's red-light district, home to five hundred "ladies of the night." Technically these brothels stood on land that was owned by St. Paul's Chapel, so the students gleefully called it the "Holy Ground."

We don't know if he ever visited the Holy Ground, but we do know that he studied anatomy and, perhaps, almost became a doctor. "I have often heard him speak of the interest and ardor he felt when prosecuting the study of anatomy," his physician later said. "Few men knew more of the structure of the human frame and its functions."

Thankfully he changed his mind. If he had focused only on medicine, it's possible that:

A) You'd be buying this book in British pounds;
B) There might not be an America;
C) This book wouldn't exist, because Hamilton wouldn't have done anything noteworthy.

(Unless, as a doctor, he somehow cured cancer. Which is unlikely, but possible.)

THE RULES FOR MR. PHILIP HAMILTON, AGE 18

What did Hamilton's average day look like? We can get a fascinating glimpse from a letter he wrote, years later, that provides his son a daily regimen:

From the first of April to the first of October he is to rise not later than Six o'clock—The rest of the year not later than Seven. If earlier he will deserve commendation. Ten will be his hour of going to bed throughout the year.

From the time he is dressed in the morning till nine o clock (the time for breakfast excepted) he is to read Law.

At nine he goes to the office & continues there till dinner time . . . After Dinner he reads law at home till five o'clock. From this hour till seven he disposes of his time as he pleases. From seven to ten he reads and studies whatever he pleases.

From twelve on Saturday he is at Liberty to amuse himself.

On Sunday he will attend the morning Church. The rest of the day may be applied to innocent recreations.

So lenient! Philip has more than *half of one day* to pursue "innocent recreations," which, knowing Hamilton, means writing a 70-page treatise about the Law.

DRINK UP THE FACTS

—

"The continent of Europe is 2,600 miles long and 2,800 miles broad."

ALL THE WORLD SEEMED to fascinate Alexander Hamilton. No detail was too small, no concept too large. As he read books to fill his brain with knowledge, he seemed hell-bent on retaining every scrap of data, as if preparing to answer every question that would ever be asked on *Jeopardy!*

At King's College he scribbled down facts that intrigued him. And then consider the notes he later took in a journal during the Revolutionary War: "The continent of Europe is 2,600 miles long and 2,800 miles broad." Okay, good to know. "The Dutch in the Greenland fishery have from 150 to 200 sails and ten thousand seamen."

No tidbit seemed too random or arcane. He jotted down infant-mortality statistics, foreign-exchange rates, the size of the British economy, the number of frigates in the French navy (twenty-four), and the key exports of Ireland ("cattle, hides, furs, tallow, butter, cheese, honey, wax, salt, hemp . . ."—it goes on for a while). Also, just in case you're curious, "the proportion for crystal glass is 200 pounds of tarso to 130 of salt."

He never abandoned the habit. Years later, as a lawyer, he compiled lists of facts, data, and Latin quotations that he could brandish in the courtroom. He sprinkled in commentary like how one witness "must have been a blockhead." He wrote the same way he did everything—fast and without hesitation.

Whether he knew it or not—and he probably did—Hamilton was stocking an arsenal of facts that he would later use to demolish his opponents. These facts would resurface in places like *The Federalist Papers,* where Hamilton casually notes that "Scotland will furnish a cogent example," and rattles off a history lesson of the Scottish clans.

In that same army notebook, Hamilton transcribed philosophical passages that helped mold his understanding of the world: "As a general marches at the head of his troops," says the Greek orator Demosthenes, politicians should "march at the head of affairs; insomuch that they ought not to wait [for] the event to know what measures to take, but the measures which they have taken, ought to produce the *event*." (Takeaway: Don't be a wimp and wait for a focus group—proceed boldly.)

Also in the army journal, he writes that in ancient Rome, "[a] husband might put away his wife for three causes: adultery, poisoning her children, and counterfeiting his keys." One of these things is not like the other . . . (To indulge in some armchair psychology: given that his own mother was tossed in jail for adultery, it's no surprise that this quote caught his eye. Wounds fester.)

He also wrote notes about sex. Or, specifically, he wrote notes about bizarre sexual practices from Plutarch's *Lives.* (Porn has come a long way.) In his journal, teenage Hamilton records that in ancient Rome, during the celebration of Lupercalia, naked married men whipped married women and "the young women were glad of this kind of whipping as they imagined it helped conception." (Brilliant. With naked whippings to aid in fertility, who needs in vitro fertilization?)

Centuries later, scientists would attempt to quantify what Hamilton knew as a teenager: Writing things down makes you smarter, and it also pays to do it by hand. A 2016 study from Princeton found that students who take *written* notes outperform those who type, as "note-taking is a pretty dynamic process," according to cognitive psychologist Michael Friedman. "You are transforming what you hear in your mind." Reading is Step 1. Retention is Step 2. So your elementary-school teacher was right: take notes.

DON'T JOIN THE CLUB, MAKE THE CLUB

—

"We ought not to be without a voice."

HAMILTON WASN'T THE KIND of college kid who locked himself in the dorm room. He quickly found like-minded students, and they even started a club. As a freshman at King's College, Hamilton created something of a Dead Poets Society, rounding up four other friends to create a "weekly club for our improvement in composition, in debating, and in public speaking," recalls club member Robert Troup, a lifelong friend. He adds that "in all the performances of the club, [Hamilton] made extraordinary displays of richness of genius and energy of mind."

Clubs like this are useful. They can serve as a safe space where you can share, swap, and debate ideas. Today, that forum might be a supportive writers group, a photography club, or a weekly breakfast with your colleagues.

Hamilton read his essays to his group, sharpening his debating skills. He also practiced giving speeches. And as the Manhattan air began to crackle with revolutionary spirit, he would soon take these skills public.

In 1774, much of New York still sympathized with King

George. (Hamilton did, after all, attend *King's* College.) Revolution was far from certain. "New York of all the major colonies was the least anxious to get into trouble with the British," explains Flexner, as "its economy was highly dependent on mercantile connections with England" and was vulnerable to British naval attack. So it took some chutzpah to rebuke the king. The radical Sons of Liberty arranged a demonstration in "The Fields," right near Hamilton's college campus—now it's City Hall Park— hoping to gin up support for boycotting British goods.

Hamilton was a spectator in the crowd. He watched all the speeches. While he must have known that he had read deeper, thought harder, and seen more clearly than the others, he didn't plan to speak up. Then, according to Hamilton's son (who heard this story years later), the people next to him in the crowd, who only knew him as the "Young West Indian," urged him to give a speech. He politely declined. (Like Vince Vaughn in *Old School*: "I'm not a talker!") But as more and more radicals gave speeches, he realized that no one was making the arguments that needed to be made.

So he spoke up. "Overawed by the scene before him, he hesitated and faltered," relates his son, but then, as he kept speaking— and surely emboldened by all the speeches he gave in his weekly club—his voice grew louder and more confident. He had found his mojo. The speech launched into a "discussion, clear, cogent, and novel, of the great principles involved in the controversy . . . and described the waves of rebellion sparkling with fire."

No transcript exists of the speech—the sole account is from his son (and some historians dispute it)—but we can imagine young

Hamilton, at last given a platform, uncorking all the arguments that had long been brewing in his head. The crowd was stunned. They looked at him in silence. *Who is this kid? Where'd he come from?* Then came a whispered murmur: "It's a collegian!" Others took up the cry. "It's a collegian!" The crowd then burst into applause at "the extraordinary eloquence of this young stranger."

Alexander Hamilton was no longer a spectator. Game on.

SEEK THE CORE PRINCIPLES

—

*"The best way of determining disputes and of
investigating truth, is by descending to elementary
principles. Any other method may only bewilder
and misguide the understanding."*

I N AN AGE BEFORE the Internet or television, the battle for
public opinion was fought, primarily, through the medium
of political pamphlets. These "pamphlets" could run 20
or 40 pages and had dense, complicated arguments that
wouldn't squeeze into 140-character tweets. And yet people read
them. People *debated* them.

And in the winter of 1774, just a few months after Hamilton's
impromptu speech, the Tories—those siding with Parliament—
made a strong case with their own pamphlets. The Tories could
smell trouble: some Bostonians had thrown a little party with
some tea, so the president of King's College, Myles Cooper, wrote
a pamphlet blasting the "illegitimate" Continental Congress, reminding New Yorkers that the "subjects of Great Britain are the
happiest people on earth" and that "the behavior of the colonies
has been intolerable."

Plenty of New Yorkers agreed. Why rock the boat?

Leading the Tory cause was a "very pompous" Oxford-educated rector named Samuel Seabury. He wrote a scathing anti-rebel pamphlet under the pseudonym "A Westchester Farmer." (He was not a farmer.) Seabury appealed to the colonists' wallets: if trade with Britain is boycotted, he warned, then farmers would feel the pinch. He asks them mockingly: "Can you live without money?"

Several patriots took up a response. Most of these were ignored. All except one.

"I am neither merchant, nor farmer . . . I address you because I wish well to my country," writes Alexander Hamilton, now just seventeen years old, still in college, under the pseudonym "A Friend to America." In a thirty-five-page manifesto, he blasted Seabury in a pamphlet called "A Full Vindication." (He was vindicating the Boston Tea Party, Continental Congress, and perhaps subconsciously, his own decision to become a patriot.)

"That Americans are entitled to freedom is incontestable on every rational principle," he begins. His eyes can see independence—and even prosperity—around the bend:

We can live without trade of any kind. Food and clothing we have within ourselves. Our climate produces cotton, wool, flax, and hemp; which, with proper cultivation, would furnish us with summer apparel.

"Summer apparel!" Even in the outbreak of a war, you can always take a moment for summer fashion.

We have sheep, which, with due care in improving and increasing them, would soon yield a sufficiency of wool. The

large quantity of skins we have among us would never let
us want a warm and comfortable suit.

Winter coats, suits, summer skirts—we've got it all, baby!

The pamphlet was a hit. Soon it began to slingshot through the colonies. "Hamilton sounded more like an experienced political philosopher than a seventeen-year-old college student," observes Newton. Since Hamilton wrote it anonymously, guessing the author's identity was a kind of parlor game. Who was this mysterious "Friend of America"? Some thought it must be a senior statesman—maybe John Jay?

Seabury accepted the challenge. The Tory wrote a 16,000-word rebuttal, mocking "A Friend to America" and charging him for having "no remedy but *artifice, sophistry, misrepresentation* and *abuse.*"

It was *on*.

Hamilton spent weeks on his rebuttal to the rebuttal, gathering research and polishing his arguments. He dug deep, emerging with an epic 32,000-word pamphlet called "The Farmer Refuted." (Hamilton had now written 60,000 words in just a couple of months. For perspective, the book you are holding clocks in at 58,000 words and, I'm embarrassed to say, took much longer.)

It was his first masterpiece. "Such is my opinion of your abilities as a critic," he tells Seabury, "that I very much prefer your disapprobation to your applause." Now he twists the knife. "I will venture to pronounce it one of the most ludicrous performances which has been exhibited to public view."

He soon drops the sarcasm and gets to business. "The Farmer

Refuted" is a more mature work. Hamilton channels a habit that would define his entire career—he seeks the core principles. Once he finds a foundation that's rock-solid, he then proceeds, point by point, to build the logical argument. *What's the heart of the argument? What really matters?* In this case the core principle, for Hamilton, is the concept of natural rights. That's the bedrock.

The sacred rights of mankind are not to be rummaged for among old parchments or musty records. They are written, as with a sun beam, in the whole volume of human nature by the hand of divinity itself and can never be erased or obscured by mortal power.

That passage could go toe-to-toe with the Declaration of Independence. It's a lovely bit of prose. He then pivots to the possibility of war, warning that even though the Americans might be outnumbered, "there is a certain enthusiasm in liberty that makes human nature rise above itself in acts of bravery and heroism."

Seeing the future, Hamilton even predicts that, in the event of a war with Britain, we would get some help from France. Bingo. Seven years later, thanks to a big assist from the French navy, this is exactly how the war played out.

"The Farmer Refuted" catapulted Hamilton into the upper tier of political essayists. More important, the pamphlets ricocheted through the colonies, galvanizing support for the coming Revolution. As one of the leaders of the Sons of Liberty is claimed to have said, "Hamilton, after these great writings, became our oracle."

2
CAREER ADVANCEMENT

MOVE QUICK

MOVE QUICK

—

"I hate procrastination."

NEW YORK STOOD ON the brink of war. The summer of 1775 saw George Washington raise his ragged army, the Continental Congress inch closer to a declaration of independence, and the patriots fire their muskets on Bunker Hill. The king was no longer in a mood to fuss around. He knew he had the most powerful navy on the planet, so he unleashed one of its most fearful warships, the *Asia,* to remind the colonists who was boss.

The *Asia* had sixty-four heavy guns. For weeks it roamed the waters of New York Harbor, its weapons pointed at the city, looking something like an Imperial Destroyer from *Star Wars.* To stand up against the *Asia,* the American fleet had, well, nothing. There was no fleet. The city stood defenseless. Washington would never have the luxury of a navy, the army had yet to arrive, and New York had very little in the way of firepower.

The city did, however, own a key stash of weapons: twenty-four cannons, located near present-day Battery Park, at the southern tip of Manhattan. As tensions grew and as the *Asia* prowled the island, one young patriot—still taking classes at King's College—

knew that if those cannons fell into British hands, the underdogs would be even more outgunned. This patriot didn't wait for an official proclamation. He took action.

On August 23, under the cloak of darkness, eighteen-year-old Hamilton joined the Sons of Liberty on a daring mission. They used ropes to haul the cannons from their exposed position by the water to a safer spot downtown, hoping to escape notice.

No such luck. The ruckus awoke the sleeping dragon of the *Asia,* which soon trained her guns on the students. British soldiers fired on the patriots. It's likely that Hamilton, carrying a musket, fired back. At least one British soldier was killed. The *Asia* launched cannonballs at the nearby Fraunces Tavern, demolishing the roof and throwing the city into a panic. (Fraunces Tavern would rebuild; it still exists today, and they'll pour you a beer for around $8.)

Explosions shook the sky. Yet Hamilton wasn't finished—he still had a job to do. "The *Asia* fired upon the city," remembers a good friend of his, Hercules Mulligan. "I was engaged in hauling off one of the cannon when Mr. H. came up and gave me his musket." Then Hamilton hauled another of the cannons to safety.

When finished, he returned to Mulligan and asked him for his musket back. Oops—Mulligan had left the gun back by the water, or, in other words, he left it in the very hot zone that the *Asia* pelted with gunfire. So what did Hamilton do? He basically turned into Chuck Norris, plunging back into danger to rescue his musket. "I told him where I had left it, and he went for it notwithstanding [that] the firing continued, with as much unconcern as if the vessel had not been there."

Whatever your job, it's unlikely that you will be in a position to steal cannons while being fired upon by British gunships. Yet the mindset is what counts. Hamilton, again and again, would take decisive action. He made the first move. This type of initiative is rewarded in both war and peace, in the eighteenth century and the twenty-first.

As his son tells us, thanks to Hamilton's bold actions with the cannons, he "was thus associated, in the minds of the people, with the first act of resistance" in New York. There are many heroes of the Revolutionary War. And there are many brilliant Founding Fathers. Yet in the Venn diagram of "Revolutionary Action Heroes" and "Influential Statesmen," Hamilton is practically by himself, joined only by George Washington.

SAY WHAT YOU BELIEVE,
NO MATTER THE COST

—

*" 'Tis my maxim to let the plain naked truth speak
for itself, and if men won't listen to it, 'tis their own
fault; they must be contented to suffer for it."*

GUNFIRE! MUSKETS! CANNONS! So had the war started?

Not quite. When we think of the Revolutionary War, we tend to imagine the entire land, en masse, rising up against the yoke of the British Empire. The messier truth is that a good chunk of the country, and especially much of aristocratic New York, was still hemming and hawing about whether to rebel. In 1775, and in the wake of the Boston Tea Party, one of these loyalists sneered that "the people of Boston are a crooked and perverse generation." This came from Myles Cooper, the president of King's College. Hamilton would know him well.

The patriots didn't care for Cooper's remarks. Bored of just writing pamphlets, the rebels drank some booze, and then they drank some more, and eventually they thought . . . *What if we teach him a lesson? What if we beat him? . . . Maybe kill him?* "Fly for your lives!" they warned Cooper and his Tory buddies, "or anticipate your doom by becoming your own executioners."

By now the rebels were drunk. The bloodthirsty crowd grabbed weapons and clubs and swarmed the campus of King's College, taunting Myles Cooper, threatening to tar and feather him and "ride him upon a rail."

Only one thing stood between the mob and Myles Cooper: Alexander Hamilton.

The "political" thing would be to join the crowd. That would burnish his revolutionary bona fides. That would endear him to the public. That would give the people what they wanted.

But that's not our man. Hamilton, again and again, would speak his mind, regardless of how much it cost him personally or politically. Hamilton raced to the top of the stairs to guard Cooper's door.

He stared at the mob. Knowing that he risked his reputation and his very life, he glared at the crowd of drunken rebels.

"YOU! SHALL! NOT! PASS!" Hamilton roared.

Or something like that—we have no idea what he actually said. But we do know that he gave an extraordinary speech. According to Robert Troup, he "proceeded with great animation and eloquence to harangue the mob . . . on the disgrace it would bring on the cause of liberty."

Using only his words to combat the hundreds of fists and clubs, Hamilton talked, and talked, and talked—the nation's first filibuster—and bought Cooper enough time to escape from a back window in his nightgown, saving the man's life.

This scene would foreshadow the battles in Hamilton's later career—he never trusted the mob . . . even if the mob was America herself. (Back then, "democracy" had a negative connotation.)

"I am always more or less alarmed at every thing which is done of mere will and pleasure without any proper authority," he explained. The man was a rebel and a renegade, but a renegade who clutched the cold steel of logic, not the hot temper of emotion. In skirmish after skirmish, he would speak his mind, no matter the consequences.

We see less extreme examples of this all the time. At work, maybe there's peer pressure to use some fuzzy accounting to create the illusion of profits. Maybe a website wants to "juke the numbers" to puff their page views for advertisers. You have two choices: you can bury your head or you can speak up.

"Men are fond of going with the stream," Hamilton observed. Yet he cut against the current. That kind of gutsy dissent might cost you in the moment, but it usually (not always) pays a longer-term dividend. There's an upside to being the contrarian voice in a meeting—you stand out. And if it backfires? You can always get a new job. You can never get a new integrity.

Or consider this: If more Wall Street bankers had followed this maxim of Hamilton's—speaking up when they saw fishy investments—would we have suffered the financial crisis of 2008?

SEE THE FOREST *AND* THE TREES

—

*"The circumstances of our country put it in
our power to evade a pitched battle."*

I N THE SPRING OF 1776, while Benjamin Franklin, Thomas
Jefferson, and John Adams were in a committee to draft the
Declaration of Independence, nineteen-year-old Alexander
Hamilton went off to war.

This wasn't his plan. (At the time he was still taking classes at
King's College.) But as soon as the fighting started, Hamilton was
like one of those heroes who, on September 12, 2001, dropped
everything to join the Marines.

And he looked good doing it. Slim, 5'7" (then an average
height), with violet-blue eyes and a boyish face that would make
the ladies swoon, Hamilton marched with a leather hat that said
"Liberty or Death." He taught himself—as always—the basics
of how to be a soldier by reading books on military tactics. He
learned so much, so quickly, that he was soon commissioned a
captain of an artillery company.

Hamilton drilled his troops hard, and his company soon became "the most beautiful model of discipline in the whole army."
The young captain seemed as comfortable in a trench as he did
in the library. One officer remembered the first time he saw

Hamilton: "I noticed a youth, a mere stripling, small, slender, almost delicate in frame, marching beside a piece of artillery, with a cocked hat pulled down over his eyes, apparently lost in thought, with his hand resting on a cannon, and every now and then patting it, as if it were a favorite horse or a pet plaything."

This was no ceremonial position; Captain Hamilton saw immediate action. In the Battle of Brooklyn—the first major fight of the Revolutionary War—the patriots, untrained and outnumbered, were thumped by the British and had to retreat to Manhattan. As Washington's army dragged its way uptown, like a Revolutionary-era version of *The Warriors,* Hamilton's artillery company provided cover.

(Fun fact: During this retreat from Manhattan, Washington wanted to burn New York City to the ground, so it couldn't be used by the British as a base of operations. Congress said thanks but no thanks. The British would occupy Wall Street for the next seven years.)

Generals began to notice Captain Hamilton. A few generals made him cushy offers to serve in their headquarters; Hamilton politely declined—he wanted to fight. The generals admired his unit's discipline, his grasp of tactics, and perhaps an underrated quality: his vision.

How would America beat the British? Hamilton had a plan:

The circumstances of our country put it in our power to evade a pitched battle. It will be better policy to harass and exhaust the soldiery by frequent skirmishes and incursions than to take the open field with them.

As a teenager, Hamilton seemed to know Washington's future strategy before Washington himself. With jaw-dropping clairvoyance, Hamilton predicted exactly how America would win the war.

The dirty little secret of the Revolution is that Washington lost more battles than he won; the victory came through "frequent skirmishes and incursions" and a sapping of the British spirit. Parliament lost the stomach and the purse for sending more troops to the quagmire of America. (Ironically, this is the same strategy used, two hundred years later, by the Vietcong and, to some extent, the insurgents in Iraq.)

There are many lessons we can take from this. It's easy to spot the virtues like bravery, discipline, and esprit de corps. Yet many officers had those qualities, too. What set Hamilton apart was his ability to view the world with a longer lens. He didn't just think about the platoon; he thought about the army. And he didn't just think about the army; he thought about the embryo that was the United States.

None of us will ratify a Constitution. None of us will land on the $10 bill. Yet we can all learn something from this mindset: In any job, we can think beyond the scope of today's immediate tasks. What's the greater concern? How do the specifics weave into the grander tapestry?

Hamilton could see the forest *and* the trees. In fact, he looked beyond the forest, widening his vision to see the hills and the cliffs and the oceans and then, in the far distance, the shores of other lands and nations. Decades and even centuries before America became a superpower, Hamilton saw its potential for greatness, as "the boundless extent of territory we possess, the wholesome temperament of our climate, the . . . fertility of our soil, the variety of our products, the [rapid] growth of our population, the industry of our countrymen" had caused "a jealousy of our dawning splendor."

FIND A WORTHY MENTOR

—

"If I am not much mistaken he has an excellent mentor."

1

777. PUT YOURSELF IN the shoes of George Washington. For starters, you're lucky to even *own* a pair of shoes, as a good chunk of your army is barefoot, hungry, unarmed, and poorly trained. And you're suffering loss after loss.

Washington needed more bullets, more troops, more bread, more everything. And the worst part? He was buried in paperwork. "At present my time is so taken up at my desk that I am obliged to neglect many other essential parts of my duty," complained the general. "It is absolutely necessary, therefore, for me to have persons that can think for me, as well as execute orders."

Enter Alexander Hamilton.

Washington put him to work as an "aide-de-camp," giving the twenty-year-old a plum double-promotion from captain to lieutenant colonel. (Quick recap: only five years earlier, Hamilton was feeding mules in the West Indies with no prospects; now he was in the general's inner circle.)

Yet the gig itself wasn't glamorous. Something of a taskmaster, Washington demanded that his aides be "confined from morning to evening" answering his mail. They wrote a hundred letters per day. Not everyone could handle the grind; one bitter young officer, Captain Aaron Burr, "despised Washington as a man of no talents . . . who could not spell a sentence of common English." Burr lasted exactly ten days.

Hamilton, on the other hand, called the general "Your Excellency," and the general called him "my boy." But he wasn't some teacher's pet whom the rest of the staff loathed. "Frank, affable, intelligent and brave, young Hamilton became the favorite of his fellow soldiers," remembered one of his friends. Hamilton was the youngest and the brightest of the aides; they called him "The Little Lion," "Ham," and "Hammie."

The Little Lion had learned a key lesson: When you see greatness, learn from it. Respect it. "For the first time in his life—also for the last—Alexander Hamilton was meeting a man who was greater than himself," suggests Brookhiser. "Hamilton's understanding was quicker than Washington's, and his analytical powers were greater. But in every other mental or moral quality, Washington was his equal or superior." Game respects game.

Learning from this mentor, Hammie was developing the skills, contacts, and reputation that would propel him to future glory. He wrote letters to Congress, serving as a link between the civilian government and the commander in chief. People learned his name. (Bonus lesson? The importance of networking. Hamilton always had a knack for making the right contacts.)

In any job and in any industry, mentors open doors, providing connections that can help you for decades. And they usually allow the scope of your job to expand beyond the official responsibilities. For example, Hamilton was never *formally* tapped as a military adviser, but insiders knew the truth. "During the whole time that he was one of the General's aides-de-camp, Hamilton had to *think* as well as to *write* for him in all his most important correspondence," recalls one general. They huddled over maps together, talked strategy, brainstormed how to beat the British.

Mentorships are long-term investments. For Hamilton and Washington, the partnership lasted twenty-two years and helped forge the nation. "Washington possessed the outstanding judgment, sterling character, and clear sense of purpose needed to guide his sometimes wayward protégé; he saw that the volatile Hamilton needed a steadying hand," reasons Chernow. "Hamilton, in turn, contributed philosophical depth, administrative expertise, and comprehensive policy knowledge that nobody in Washington's ambit ever matched. He could transmute wispy ideas into detailed plans and turn revolutionary dreams into enduring realities. As a team, they were unbeatable and far more than the sum of their parts."

"HAMILTON. ALEXANDER HAMILTON."

Hamilton was secretly a spy.

Okay, that's not entirely accurate, but he did have a role in Washington's ring of spies, a shadowy organization that helped win the war.

As the general's most trusted aide-de-camp, Hamilton helped coordinate the secret agents, issue orders, decipher coded messages, and even recruit young officers. It's likely that he recruited his old pal from King's College, Hercules Mulligan, who then went deep undercover as a tailor in New York.

For more than six years, while mocked by his neighbors as a British sympathizer, Mulligan secretly gathered intelligence and sent it to headquarters. It's possible that he foiled a plot to assassinate Washington. "Although little known to most Americans, Hercules Mulligan, if even a small fraction of the stories is true, is one of the unsung heroes of the American Revolution," explains Newton.

How important was Hercules Mulligan? In 1981, the director of the CIA considered erecting him a statue; in fact, he wanted Mulligan's statue to *replace* the one of legendary Nathan Hale. The rationale? Hale got caught. Mulligan didn't. The CIA director noted that Mulligan "functioned throughout the war, was never caught, never broke his cover, and rests today, still well covered, in the churchyard of Trinity Church facing Wall Street." On the bright side for Nathan Hale: if they did topple his statue, technically he would be giving two lives for his country.

PICK UP THE SLACK

—

*"I will stay with you, my dear General, and die
with you! Let us all die rather than retreat!"*

THE WINTER OF 1777. Valley Forge. Hamilton shivered with the rest of the army. He looked around and saw troops who were cold, hungry, unpaid, and without jackets or blankets. Soldiers starved; soldiers died. Why were there so many shortages? Congress was impotent. The Continental Congress had no real ability to raise funds—they couldn't tax—so they failed to provide enough food, boots, or bullets.

From the diary of a soldier who lived through it: "Poor food-hard lodging-cold weather-fatigue—nasty clothes—nasty cookery—vomit half my time—smoked out of my senses—the devil's in it—I can't endure it . . . There comes a bowl of beef soup—full of burnt leaves and dirt."

Colonel Hamilton saw all of this and began thinking, planning, strategizing. Someday he would do something about it.

In the meantime, the army had nothing to do but train and drill. Somehow, at the end of that winter, they emerged with a new steel and discipline. The weather grew sunnier and so did their confidence. It was time to test-drive this new American fighting machine.

An opportunity soon presented itself, as the British army, ten thousand strong, wormed its way north of Philadelphia in a long column that stretched for miles. It seemed ripe for attack. But how?

The council of war was split. Hamilton (now twenty-one), who was keeping minutes at the meeting, favored a bold attack. ("I hold it an established maxim, that there is three to one in favor of the party attacking.") Others agreed. General Charles Lee, however, thought that an attack would be too dangerous, and he proposed a more modest plan that, as Hamilton later put it, was so cautious that it would "have done honor to the most honorable society of midwives, and to them only."

Washington listened to both sides and eventually agreed with Hamilton: *Attack*. He put Lee in charge, but Lee, who never liked the plan, politely declined. Then Lee changed his mind and said he'd do it. Then he changed his mind again. Finally, Lee said he'd do it, *this time for real*.

Washington ordered an attack pending "favorable circumstances." But what does that mean, exactly? What counts as "favorable"? It was Hamilton's job to find out. He joined his friend the Marquis de Lafayette—the French aristocrat who had famously volunteered without pay—on a two-man reconnaissance mission.

They rode for days, pulling all-nighters and sweating in the 90-degree heat, then split up to cover more ground. Hamilton had now fully evolved from scribe to strategist, so he analyzed the board and put the chess pieces in play. Soon he found the right terrain for the right moment and informed Washington, who ordered Lee to attack.

In what would later be known as the Battle of Monmouth, Washington had the enemy in his crosshairs. Lee now led a smaller force of eight hundred advance troops; his job was to engage the British. Together, Hamilton and Washington waited at headquarters, their ears straining to hear the sound of cannons and muskets. Only silence. Then came the sound of hoofbeats. A horse raced toward them. American soldiers fled from the battlefield, panicked, rushing back toward Washington. This made no sense, as the battle hadn't even started.

"By God, they are flying from a shadow!" one officer said.

The entire operation was about to unravel. The entire army was now at risk. A furious Washington galloped to the site of the battle—or rather lack of battle—and barked at General Lee.

"What is the meaning of this, sir?" Washington roared, courteous as always. "I desire to know the meaning of this disorder and confusion!"

"The American troops would not stand the British bayonets," said Lee.

"You damn poltroon, you never tried them!" Washington yelled.

Hamilton jumped into the fray. Not fretting about his "official responsibilities" or his "job description," he immediately picked up General Lee's slack. "I saw some pieces of artillery pretty advantageously posted," he later remembered, so he rallied the fleeing troops and barked out orders.

Colonel Hamilton grabbed a bayonet and ordered a charge. He approached General Lee and cried out in passion, "I will stay with you, my dear General, and die with you! Let us all die rather than retreat!"

This isn't some apocryphal myth. Multiple witnesses heard Hamilton yell this—including Lee himself, who later remembered that Hamilton cried out, "That's right, my dear General, and I will stay and we will all die here on the spot." Not intending it as a compliment, he later said that Hamilton was in "a sort of frenzy of valor." (The general quickly clarified that "it is not that sort of valor [that] will ever be of any great use to the community.")

Death greeted Hamilton and gave him a flirtatious kiss, as his horse was shot from underneath him and he tumbled to the ground. The injuries would keep him bedridden for weeks. (*See you on the dueling grounds,* Death said with a laugh.)

It was a stunning display of military courage. Yet Hamilton deflected the praise and heaped it on Washington. "I never saw the General to so much advantage," Hamilton later remembered. "His coolness and firmness were admirable . . . He directed the whole with the skill of a master workman."

Hamilton didn't write of his own daring soldiery, but others did. "I am happy to have it in my power to mention the merit of your young friend Hamy," wrote John Laurens, another aide-de-camp, and Hamilton's most intimate friend. Laurens thought the aides had "proved themselves as worthy to wield the sword as the pen."

Others took notice, too. "Hamilton's exploits [were] published in *The Pennsylvania Packet* on July 16, 1778," writes Michael Newton. "The whole country had now heard of Alexander Hamilton and his courage under fire."

Hamilton had picked up the slack. And the legend was growing.

HAMILTON'S FIRST DUEL

On a cold winter afternoon in December 1778, Hamilton had his first taste of dueling. He served as a right-hand man, or "second," for John Laurens in a duel against Charles Lee. The dispute? After his embarrassing retreat at Monmouth, Lee had talked some trash and somehow blamed *Washington* for the blunder, calling his inner circle—among other unspeakable insults—a bunch of "earwigs" and "toad eaters." That could not stand.

Dueling was common in the army. Honor was hard currency, and if a man insulted your honor, the only acceptable option was to challenge him to a duel. Most duels were not fatal; one study showed that "only" 20 percent of duels ended in death.

Lee and Laurens met in the woods near Philadelphia. (Incidentally, the second for Charles Lee was *not* Aaron Burr. Works nicely in the musical, though.)

The two men loaded their pistols, walked ten paces apart, stared at each other, then fired.

Laurens's shot hit its target. Lee's did not. No one was killed. This settled the affair. Both men left the field with their lives and their honor intact. "Upon the whole," Hamilton said in good cheer, "we think it a piece of justice to the two gentlemen to declare that after they met, their conduct was strongly marked with all the politeness, generosity, coolness, and firmness that ought to characterize a transaction of this nature." This dueling thing is great! Maybe he'd get to try it.

EXIT WITH CLASS

—

"The great man and I have come to an open rupture."

B Y 1781, HAMILTON AND WASHINGTON had been side by side for more than four years. At times they slept in the same room. By then Hammie had written countless letters, negotiated prisoner exchanges, written more letters, crossed the Delaware, helped train the army, heard the man snore, and written still more letters.

The novelty had worn off. Like anyone stuck in the same job for years with no promotion in sight, Hamilton thought about quitting. He was chained to a desk and he longed to lead men into battle. "I have no passion for scribbling," he complained to a friend, which, given his twenty-seven volumes of letters, is kind of hilarious.

Can I go fight? he asked Washington.

No.

Please?

No.

Finally he could take no more. On February 16, 1781, Hamilton and Washington had a falling-out. This happens in the workplace. Bosses grate on your nerves, rifts happen, and feelings get bruised.

If this were a movie, the two would clash in some epic, manly showdown with lots of heavy breathing and clenched fists. (This is basically what happens in the musical: *"Call me* <u>Son</u> *one more time!"*) In real life, however, the trigger was almost comically mundane.

As Hamilton lays it out, Washington had asked to speak to him. *Sure!* he said, but first he had to take care of something. (Urgent business with Lafayette.) Then he immediately reported back to the general, meeting him at the top of a staircase. And then, according to Hamilton's letter, the two men spoke these very words:

WASHINGTON: Colonel Hamilton, you have kept me waiting at the head of the stairs these ten minutes. I must tell you, sir, you treat me with disrespect.

HAMILTON: I am not conscious of it, sir; but since you have thought it necessary to tell me so, we part.

WASHINGTON: Very well, sir, if it be your choice.

And that was that. Hamilton decided to leave Washington's inner circle. He later insists that "my absence, which gave so much umbrage, did not last two minutes."

Hamilton, by now, felt that he was being punished for his own competence. Other, less talented aides had been granted commissions to lead troops in battle—but not Hamilton. Other motivations? Armchair psychologists love to theorize that since Hamilton lacked a father figure, the two had a father/son dynamic full of topsy-turvy emotions, but most historians have debunked that reading. (There were even some goofy theories that Hamilton was secretly Washington's illegitimate son, but they have about as much proof as the Obama/Kenya Birther movement.)

Whatever the reasons, Hamilton quit. And in fairness to him, he had already served for nearly five years, longer than most officers. He had put in his time. (For example, Colonel Aaron Burr had retired two years earlier, in 1779, and now he enjoyed a head start in his legal career.)

Workplace conflict is inevitable; the trick is how you deal with it. There are two options:

1) Leave in a huff.
2) Exit with class.

Hamilton took the latter route. He vowed to keep the rift a secret to preserve the general's sterling reputation. He put in his two weeks' notice—two *months,* actually—maintained his composure, and patiently waited for his replacement. For the rest of his career he remained loyal to Washington, never once criticizing him in public.

And while Hamilton had left Washington's inner circle, he had not resigned his commission. (If he had left on bad terms, that window would be closed.) He bided his time. He kept lobbying Washington to let him fire his musket.

He would soon get his chance.

GO TO WAR FOR YOUR PROMOTION

—

"Regular promotion is the only means by which these gentlemen can, or ought to expect to rise into eminence."

HAMILTON DID NOT REMAIN IDLE. No longer working in Washington's headquarters, he used his "downtime" to crank out a suite of political essays, "The Continentalist," which outlined his future vision for the United States. (He wrote this while the nation was still at war! His move is reminiscent of some other great leaders during World War II: even before D-day, with victory far from clinched, FDR and Churchill sketched a postwar plan for dealing with Stalin.)

Then Colonel Hamilton put down his quill and grabbed his bayonet. More than two hundred years before the world had heard of Sheryl Sandberg, Alexander Hamilton Leaned In. He did not wait for the promotion. He went to war for it.

He was rejected.

So he asked again.

And again.

And again. "It has become necessary to me to apply to your Excellency to know in what manner . . . you will be able to employ me in the ensuing campaign," he wrote Washington. "I am ready to enter into activity whenever you think proper."

Fine, Washington decided, and only after this relentless lobbying, on July 31, 1781, he gave Hamilton the command of an infantry battalion.

Let's zoom out a bit: For years the plucky rebels had bided their time—practically inventing guerrilla warfare—and had, for the most part, dodged massive army-on-army battles. (It's the exact strategy that Hamilton had predicted.) Now, finally, the patriots had the edge. Washington knew that Britain's largest army, led by General Cornwallis, was hemmed in at Yorktown, Virginia.

Cornwallis's army was no joke. Earlier in the year, he had stormed Virginia and marched on Charlottesville, forcing the state's government to evacuate. Virginia's governor, terrified, galloped away on a horse. The governor's actions were questionable at best, cowardly at worst, and prompted an investigation of conduct. (The governor's name was Thomas Jefferson. It's the closest he would ever get to combat.)

Washington joined forces with Lafayette, and together they assembled fifteen thousand soldiers at Williamsburg, near Yorktown. The general surveyed the scene: Cornwallis had dug into his position, building defensive walls around his army, hoping to buy time until the British navy could sail to his rescue.

The British had erected ten redoubts, or temporary forts, to guard the perimeter, erecting makeshift walls to shield against the looming cannon fire. To puncture the heart of Cornwallis's army, the patriots would need to capture these redoubts. Everything depended on capturing Redoubt #10, the one closest to the Americans.

For days the armies traded cannon fire, the skies shaking with thunder. Washington personally launched the first cannon. One surviving British officer later remembered seeing "men lying nearly everywhere who were mortally wounded, whose heads, arms, and legs had been shot off."

Yet cannon fire alone wouldn't finish the job. They needed Redoubt #10. If successful, this attack would cripple Cornwallis's army and win the war.

Guess who Washington put in charge?

Jean-Joseph Sourbader de Gimat.

Are you freaking kidding me? Hamilton must have thought. So again he pushed for the promotion. He made a case to Washington that he had seniority, that he was technically the officer of the day (i.e., it was his turn in the rotation), and that he had dibs.

Washington agreed. He rewarded his star protégé, and a joyous Hamilton went back to his tent and shouted, "We have it! We have it!" (In the musical, Washington implores Hamilton to answer the call of duty and lead the attack; the reality was basically the reverse.)

Before the siege itself, Hamilton's men dug a trench to further trap the redcoats. When the trench was complete, he ordered his troops—in full view of the British army!—to execute crisp parade drills, marching back and forth, essentially flipping King George the bird.

Then he drew up the battle plans. Not only would Hamilton's men lead the attack, they would do so without any bullets. The mission relied on speed, silence, and audacity. The soldiers emptied their rifles and fixed their bayonets, ensuring the conflict would be bloody and quiet. Just to repeat: *Hamilton and his men would race into battle without bullets*. This also foreshadowed the strategy that would be used, many years later, against zombies in *The Walking Dead*.

Perhaps Hamilton gave his men a pep talk. Perhaps he huddled with his good friend John Laurens. Perhaps he wrote 50,000 words to calm the nerves. On the night of the siege, Colonel Alexander Hamilton, his bayonet fixed, waited in the trench for a signal. He stared at the sky. Waiting. Waiting. Waiting.

Then it came: a burst of artillery that lit the night's sky. He leaped from the trench. His men followed. He sprinted the length of two football fields, his bayonet flashing, between the trench and the British fort.

The redoubt's wall had pointy sticks meant to impale the invaders, so Hamilton, once his troops caught up, climbed up the back of one of his men and leaped over the wall. His men followed. They were shot at. He ordered his men to scream like animals, and as one soldier later recalled, "[t]hey made such a terrible yell . . . that one believed the whole wild hunt had broken out."

It was over in a heartbeat. Hamilton's troops had the element of surprise and quickly routed the British. Some of his men wanted to kill the defeated redcoats, but Hamilton ensured mercy, later saying that "the soldiers spared every man who ceased to resist."

This effectively ended the Battle of Yorktown, and that victory, in turn, effectively ended the War of Independence. With Redoubt #10 captured, Washington could now complete a massive trench that choked off Cornwallis's army, letting him pummel the Brits with impunity.

Colonel Alexander Hamilton had rewarded Washington's trust, won the hearts of his troops, and become a legitimate war hero. The majestic British Empire had just been brought to its knees, and as the fallen redcoats trudged away, a marching band played the tune "The World Turned Upside Down."

3
ROMANCE

SEDUCE WITH YOUR STRENGTHS

SEDUCE WITH YOUR STRENGTHS

—

" 'ALL FOR LOVE' is my motto."

W E LIKE TO IMAGINE that the Founding Fathers were these grim, wise, sober men who pondered the Big Truths, but even philosophers have certain needs—and young Hamilton was an unabashed flirt. (Don't forget his poetry: "Celia's an artful little slut.")

In his courtship of the ladies of New York, Hamilton wisely refrained from blurting out things like "The continent of Europe is 2,600 miles long and 2,800 miles broad" or "The proportion for crystal glass is 200 pounds of tarso to 130 of salt." Instead, he played to his strengths: writing and oration.

Shortly after moving to New York, Hamilton was smitten by the beautiful Kitty Livingston, so he wrote her a bold letter:

I challenge you to meet me in whatever path you dare. And, if you have no objection, for variety and amusement, we will even make excursions in the flowery walks and roseate bowers of Cupid. You know I am renowned for <u>gallantry</u> and shall always be able to entertain you with a choice collection of the prettiest things imaginable.

(The word "gallantry" doesn't quite mean what you think it means here. Back then it had one clear connotation: sex.)

Hamilton even made time for gallantry, of all places, in the Revolutionary War. It's true that much of the war was cold, wet, dark, and bloody. Yet it's also true that for the inner circle of Washington's advisers, at times, there were pockets of culture, parties, and even high society.

To boost morale, Martha Washington threw balls and dinner parties for the young officers like Hamilton, John Laurens, Aaron Burr, and Lafayette. Fashionable ladies joined—they were called "camp ladies." (When future chief justice John Marshall saw the party scene, he said, "Never was I a witness to such a scene of lewdness.")

Hamilton splurged for a subscription to a "dancing assembly" that met during the winter lulls in fighting. Surely benefiting from his skills of oration, he also flirted with the farmers' daughters. As one officer wrote in his journal:

> *A rainy evening. Let me see what company we have indoors. A pretty, full-faced, youthful, playful lass, and a family of Quakers, meek and unsuspicious. Hamilton, thou shalt not tread this ground! I mark it for myself.*

"Hamilton's love-making was evidently pursued with the same activity as everything else he did," sighed his grandson. Not everyone put it so kindly. John Adams blasted "his audacious and unblushing attempts upon ladies of the highest rank and purest virtue." Benjamin Latrobe called him "an insatiable libertine."

And we can only imagine what Hamilton said to make Abigail

Adams blush. "Oh, I have read his heart in his wicked eyes," wrote Abigail. "The very devil is in them. They are lasciviousness itself." (And while it's a delightful anecdote that Martha Washington named her tomcat Hamilton, alas, this has been roundly debunked.)

There's not much proof, if any, that Hamilton ever *acted* on any of these flirtations. But he had that kind of rep—and his enemies exploited it. Especially John Adams, who said he had "debauched morals." Still not clear enough? Adams says—and it's a shame Twitter wasn't around then—that Hamilton had "a superabundance of secretions which he could not find whores enough to draw off."

KNOW WHAT YOU WANT,
GET WHAT YOU NEED

—

"She must be young, handsome (I lay most
stress upon a good shape . . .)"

H, HAMILTON. HOW HE MUST REGRET this letter.
When he was twenty-two years old, he wrote to
his best friend and fellow aide-de-camp, John
Laurens, clarifying precisely what he was looking
for in a partner.

His note begins:

She must be young, handsome (I lay most stress upon a
good shape), sensible (a little learning will do), well-
bred . . . chaste and tender (I am an enthusiast in my no-
tions of fidelity and fondness) . . .

In other words, she needs to be hot. Good body. No need for
Harvard or anything, but she can't be an idiot. Oh, and also? It'd
be nice if she's rich. He continues:

. . . of some good nature, a great deal of generosity (she
must neither love money nor scolding, for I dislike equally
a termagant and an economist).

This is the best part. Her personality can be mediocre (of "some good nature"), but she needs to be really, really generous, even though she, herself, doesn't care about money.

In politics, I am indifferent what side she may be of; I think I have arguments that will easily convert her to mine.

Actually, *that's* the best part.

As to religion, a moderate streak will satisfy me. She must believe in god and hate a saint.

Fair enough.

But as to fortune, the larger stock of that the better. You know my temper and circumstances and will therefore pay special attention to this article in the treaty.

Just in case you missed it! She needs to be rich.

Though I run no risk of going to purgatory for my avarice, yet as money is an essential ingredient to happiness in this world—as I have not much of my own and as I am very little calculated to get more either by my address or indus- try—it must needs be that my wife, if I get one, bring at least a sufficiency to administer to her own extravagancies.

For a *third time* he stresses the point. Rich, rich, rich.
So what do we make of all this? The letter has vexed the Ham-

ilton clan for centuries. When writing a biography, his son, likely horrified, scribbled the note "I must not publish the whole of this" and nixed the parts about the money.

On the one hand, Hamilton was only twenty-two years old. He later suggests to Laurens that he's just messing around: "Do I want a wife? No— I have plagues enough without desiring to add to the number that greatest of all." Besides, think back to when you were younger. Imagine all the things you said about your crushes and fantasies. Now imagine every single throwaway joke of yours—no matter how embarrassing—standing the test of time. Hamilton, surely, did not foresee that this letter would be scrutinized for two hundred years. Immortality has its drawbacks.

Then again . . . Hamilton likely put some real thought into the personality of whom he would marry. Remember his own troubled childhood? He saw firsthand the unhappiness of his own parents on St. Croix, once remarking, "It's a dog's life when two dissonant tempers meet." He knew the value of getting a marriage right.

And he would soon meet a woman who checked every box on his Wife List.

LOVE WITHOUT LABELS

—

*"I wish, my Dear Laurens, it might be in my power, by
action rather than words to convince you that I love you."*

WASHINGTON'S INNER CIRCLE WAS a tight-knit
group. Furiously scribbling the general's correspondence, these aides-de-camp tended to
work in one building, eat at one table, sleep in
the same farmhouse—sometimes two to a bed.

Hamilton was especially close with John Laurens. A man of culture from South Carolina, Laurens was trim, well read, intelligent,
a passionate abolitionist, and beautiful. Laurens had studied in
Geneva, where his courses included a Hamiltonian mix of "Latin,
Greek, Italian, belle lettres, physics, history, geography, mathematics, experimental philosophy, fencing, riding, and civil law."

Hamilton's friendship with Laurens was perhaps the most
intimate of his life. Just how intimate? The question has titil-
lated historians for centuries. (And, more recently, the Internet.)
"There was a deep fondness of friendship, which approached the
tenderness of feminine attachment," notes Hamilton's son. His
grandson picked up on the same vibe, sensing "a note of romance
in their friendship, quite unusual even in those days."

Was Hamilton bisexual?

Consider his letter to Laurens:

Cold in my professions, warm in friendships, I wish, my dear Laurens, it might be in my power, by action rather than words, to convince you that I love you . . . I hardly knew the value you had taught my heart to set upon you.

It's downright steamy. He continues:

Indeed, my friend, it was not well done. You know the opinion I entertain of mankind and how much it is my desire to preserve myself free from particular attachments, and to keep my happiness independent of the caprice of others. You should not have taken advantage of my sensibility to steal into my affections without my consent.

Then, in other letters, he sounds like the guy who freaks out because his girlfriend isn't texting enough, complaining to Laurens that:

I have written you five or six letters since you left Philadelphia . . . But, like a jealous lover, when I thought you slighted my caresses, my affection was alarmed and my vanity piqued.

The two soldiers welcomed a third into their bromance: Lafayette. As Hamilton's grandson tells us, "The gay trio to which Hamilton and Laurens belonged was made complete by Lafayette."

They swapped letters laced with subtext that could, well, go either way. "Before this campaign, I was your friend and very intimate friend, agreeable to the ideas of the world," Lafayette wrote, confiding that "my sentiment has increased to such a point the world knows nothing about."

It's totally possible—and likely probable—that this was just brotherly love. Then again, what do we make of this next one? Also in the same "what I want in a partner" letter to John Laurens, Hamilton concluded that he was mostly just messing around as an excuse to write a longer letter, as a way of "lengthening out the only kind of intercourse now in my power."

Sly double entendre, or a reach? While some have pounced on the word "intercourse," consider the historical context: back then the word was often used, quite innocently, to describe routine correspondence. From George Washington: "we have kept up a regular and friendly intercourse"; "the less intercourse they have with the troops the better"; and ". . . friendly intercourse with your honorable body." *Juicy.* Except in this case, "honorable body" is the body of the Massachusetts General Court. See how easy it is to take things out of context?

Plus, platonic "manly love" really was the norm back then. Washington once referred to Lafayette as "the man I love." When the general gave Lafayette a hug, according to one eyewitness, the Frenchman "opened both his arms as wide as he could reach and caught the General round his body, hugged him as close as it was possible, and absolutely *kissed him from ear to ear* once or twice, as well as I can recollect, with as much ardor as ever an absent lover kissed his mistress on his return."

It's also worth remembering the obvious: in the Revolutionary era, there was absolutely nothing revolutionary about gay rights. The world was ruled by white men—straight white men. (One politician said that his opponent "dances with, and kisses (*filthy beast!*) those of his own sex.") "In all thirteen colonies, sodomy had been a capital offense, so if Hamilton and Laurens did become lovers—and it is impossible to say this with any certainty—they would have taken extraordinary precautions," Chernow carefully concludes. "At the very least, we can say that Hamilton developed something like an adolescent crush on his friend."

Was he? Wasn't he? We'll likely never know. But does it matter? Even if he never codified this in writing, Hamilton reminds us of an important lesson: not every relationship needs to fall into a neat category of "romantic" or "platonic buddy." The labels are irrelevant. Love takes many forms.

Hamilton was unafraid to love—in whatever capacity—his dear friend John Laurens. At the very least, this gave him a solid friendship in the midst of war. And after his mother died and his father left, Hamilton surely must have been grateful for a companion. He opened up. Unclenched his heart. It's not important that we label, categorize, or analyze. It's just important that we love.

THE LADIES OF AARON BURR

Whether he knew it or not, Hamilton had a rival for the ladies of New York City. And when it comes to the sheer number of romantic conquests, there's little doubt that Aaron Burr won this duel. Trim, poised, and handsome, Burr had dark, piercing eyes that could drill right into your soul.

Aaron Burr "was an unabashed sexual enthusiast from puberty, and he enjoyed the close companionship of dozens if not hundreds of women," writes John Sedgwick. "As a single man on the prowl, Burr distinguished between the eligible, the ineligible, and those for hire—but then had all three."

Burr recorded the details of each conquest in a sex diary, "so he could savor them all again later, like a botanist thrilled with every detail of some rare woodland flower he'd spotted years ago and pressed into a book."

The lothario eventually married an older woman, Theodosia Prevost, who charmed him with her mind and love of books. She once told him, "Your opinion of Voltaire pleases me." (Bonus factoid: James Monroe tried to seduce Theodosia as well, and when she chose Burr instead, the future president called her "the most unreasonable creature in existence.") Yet Theodosia died when Burr was still in his thirties, so he resumed his bachelor ways. He would seduce women deep into his sixties and even seventies. "He looked longingly on a woman of sixty-three, dubbing her the best-looking woman of that age he'd ever seen, and he lusted for one 'she-animal,'" notes Sedgwick.

He later boasted of these sexual escapades to his daughter, commenting on women like "[t]he chambermaid, fat, not bad; *muse* again." ("Muse" did not refer to Burr being inspired to write poetry, but was a French term referring to "an animal's rutting period.") When in France he noted: "From across the hall, the maid came. *Muse*. I couldn't send her back."

As for Hamilton? He had no need for conquests or chambermaids. He was about to meet his game changer.

FLATTER YOUR WAY TO HER HEART

—

*"My Betsey's soul speaks in every line and bids me be
the happiest of mortals. I am so and will be so."*

Meet Eliza Schuyler. She fits every single criterion of Hamilton's "What I Want in a Partner" letter. A contemporary describes her as a "brunette with the most good-natured, lively dark eyes that I ever saw, which threw a beam of good temper and benevolence over her whole countenance." One portrait shows dark eyes, fair skin, and a plunging neckline that would steal the show at the Met Gala.

Hamilton fell for Eliza hard. "I love you more and more every hour," he confessed. He wrote to her again and again, piling on the flattery the way he would later pile on the legal arguments for a national bank. He even wrote her poetry. One poem was called "Answer to the Inquiry Why I Sighed," which, it must be said, shows why he became more famous for financial reform than for love sonnets:

*Before no mortal ever knew
A love like mine so tender, true,
Completely wretched—you away,*

And but half blessed e'en while you stay.

. . .

No joy unmixed my bosom warms
But when my angel's in my arms.

One friend noted that "Hamilton is a gone man." He was so smitten, in fact, that one night when he came back from Eliza's and returned to the army's base, he had completely forgotten the password for entry. A letter that he sent to her sister gives just a glimpse of his flattery campaign:

> *I have already confessed the influence your sister has gained over me—yet notwithstanding this, I have some things of a very serious and heinous nature to lay to her charge.*

Here we can imagine him pausing for comedic effect before he levels the "charge":

> *She is most unmercifully handsome and so perverse that she has none of those petty affectations which are the prerogatives of beauty. Her good sense is destitute of that happy mixture of vanity and ostentation . . . In short she is so strange a creature, that she possesses all the beauties virtues and graces of her sex without any of those amiable defects . . .*

He flattered Eliza, he flattered her sisters, he flattered her father. Writing to his prospective mother-in-law, he said:

> *May I hope, madam, you will not consider it as a mere pro-*
> *fession when I add that, though I have not the happiness of*
> *a personal acquaintance with you, I am no stranger to the*
> *qualities which distinguish your character.*

Like a proper gentleman, Hamilton asked her father's permission for marriage; he said yes, and seemed happy to overlook the immigrant's dicey background. Clearly Philip Schuyler, a general in the army and a political heavyweight, saw potential in the kid. He wrote to Eliza that his "beloved Hamilton . . . affords me happiness too exquisite for expression . . . He is considered, as he certainly is, the ornament of his country." They tied the knot on December 14, 1780.

Even *after* the wedding Hamilton continued the flattery, gushing:

> *I am happy only when my moments are devoted to some*
> *office that respects you. I would give the world to be able*
> *to tell you all I feel and all I wish, but consult your own*
> *heart and you will know mine. What a world will soon be*
> *between us!*

The takeaway? When we find the person we want to marry, we don't need complicated dating rules and we don't need to play "the game." He didn't worry about coming on too strong. Hamilton understood a very basic tenet of human nature that, at times, we forget when we overthink, overanalyze, and overcomplicate matters of the heart: people really like to be complimented. Sometimes the basics work.

FLIRT WITH THE LINE ...
BUT NEVER CROSS IT

—

"You must be a very naughty girl indeed . . ."

Eliza Schuyler came with several perks:

1) Rich family.
2) Political connections.
3) A mansion in Albany that would serve, effectively, as his first home since his mother died on the island of St. Croix.
4) Beautiful sisters.

Let's focus on the sisters. The era's top authority on feminine charms, Benjamin Franklin, once visited the Schuyler family and praised the "lively behavior of the young ladies." They strummed the guitar, they sang, they could talk politics or history or poetry, they flirted, and they all loved Alexander Hamilton.

He first visited their wealthy estate during the war, cutting a dashing figure in his blue uniform. The youngest sister later recalled that he had a "nose of the Grecian mold, a dark bright eye, and the line of a mouth expressing decision and courage . . . the contour of a face never to be forgotten."

One sister, of course, would never forget his face: Angelica. Just a year older than Eliza, Angelica was deeply read, fluent in

French, and obsessed with gossip and politics—Hamilton's ideal sparring partner.

Their mutual infatuation was an open secret. Angelica wrote to her sister about "my *Amiable,* by my Amiable you know that I mean your Husband, for I love him very much and if you were as generous as the old Romans, you would lend him to me for a little while."

Lend him to me for a while? She's a firecracker. An incestuous harem is pushing the envelope for HBO, much less 1780. These types of letters continued for years. Angelica married a rich bore who dragged her to London, but she continued to pine for Hamilton from across the ocean. It was borderline scandalous. His political enemies would later gossip about their lovefest, as John Adams said that Hamilton's "fornications, adulteries and his *incests* were propagated far and wide."

Yet there's no proof that anything actually happened—just innuendo and hints. His grandson concedes that they had a "sprightly correspondence" that "bristles with badinage, and to many suggests the existence of a more tender feeling than would appear to be conventional, but an inspection of his whole life and hers disproves this."

Hamilton flirted and provoked and teased, but he seemed to know precisely how far he could tiptoe to the line without crossing it. (He *usually* knew this lesson. Later in life, of course, he would not always follow it.)

He also, unwittingly, provides solid advice for what married people should do if they're smitten with someone else: bring things back to the family. Invoke your spouse. If your text messages with a "friend" get a little too hot, use your partner for a bucket of cold water. ("Oh, hey, maybe the three of us should grab coffee next week.") This keeps things safely on the side of propriety.

For example, Hamilton writes to Angelica that:

Betsey and myself make you the last theme of our conversation at night and the first in the morning. We talk of you; we praise you and we pray for you.

It's a subtle reminder: *Hey, this is sexy and all, but I've got a wife. Oh, and she happens to be your sister.*

Then again, it's also true that Hamilton once referred to them as "my beautiful brunettes." It doesn't take a scholar to imagine Hamilton's fantasies . . .

4
MONEY

CONQUER THE CREDIT

CONVICTIONS FIRST, CASH SECOND

—

*"I would never again take up a cause in which
I was convinced I ought not to prevail."*

I N 1781 AND AT the close of the war, twenty-four-year-old
Alexander Hamilton now had the swashbuckling cachet of
a war hero, street cred as a revolutionary, fame as a political
essayist, and a loving wife in Eliza. He did not, however,
have a job.

So he thought about what he was good at—logic, writing,
debating—and looked for the jobs that paid handsomely. And
then he did the same thing that every philosophy and compara-
tive literature major has done for hundreds of years: he became
a lawyer.

At the time, "law school" didn't yet really exist, so most students needed a three-year apprenticeship under a practicing attorney, and perhaps years of cramming for the bar. Hamilton?
He did all of this in six months. No legal textbooks existed, so
he wrote his own: a 177-page compendium called *Practical Pro-
ceedings in the Supreme Court of the State of New York.* (This
homemade textbook was so masterful, notes Brookhiser, that it
"became the basis for study guides in the next century.")

There were only thirty-five licensed lawyers in New York City, or "one twelfth the number of prostitutes"—so he instantly joined an exclusive club. With Eliza and his new baby infant, Philip, he moved into his new digs at 57 Wall Street. "I have been employed for the last ten months in rocking the cradle and studying the art of fleecing my neighbors," he joked to Lafayette.

Let's look at two quick cases that tell us plenty about Alexander Hamilton:

1) THE FAN THIEF

EARLY IN HIS CAREER, A WOMAN stole a fan. (Hey, it's hot in the summer.) She was guilty; Hamilton defended her anyway, telling the jury that "woman is weak and requires the protection of man." Oof. No one has ever called Alexander Hamilton the Father of Women's Rights. Yet he razzle-dazzled the jury and somehow won: *Not Guilty.*

This victory—for a client who *shouldn't* have won—gnawed at Hamilton's conscience. After that rare blemish to his integrity, he resolved that "I would never again take up a cause in which I was convinced I ought not to prevail." From then onward, he did something unthinkable by today's legal standards: he only represented clients he thought to be innocent. Craziness! (In contrast, just down the street, Aaron Burr believed that "the law . . . is whatever is successfully argued and plausibly maintained.")

Another case of conviction, this one a little trickier:

2) THE EVIL TORIES

HAMILTON LOVED TO FIGHT FOR THE underdog. And in the war's aftermath, no one—not even a slave owner—was more unpopular than the Tories, those old Loyalists to the British Crown. (Remember Myles Cooper, the dude whose life Hamilton saved back in college?) Tories were spat on, beaten, tarred and feathered, and asked to leave Manhattan.

Hamilton urged for reconciliation: *Treat our enemies with respect and dignity.* He wrote papers to defend the Tories, arguing that if a mob is allowed to seek vengeance, then "no man can be safe, nor know when he may be the innocent victim of a prevailing faction." Almost overnight, his image flipped from Revolutionary Hero to British Sympathizer.

This all came to a head in the courtroom.

During the war, some evil British soldiers had confiscated a New Yorker's home, damaged the property, and even burned down a brewery. It didn't help that the brewery's owner, Mrs. Elizabeth Rutgers, was a sympathetic widow. She sued the Brits for damages.

Death to the Brits! the city cried.

Make 'em pay!

Give us more beer!

Guess who Hamilton represented?

He pointed out something no one else wanted to hear: the lawsuit hinged on the Trespass Act, which, crucially, was a *state* law. It let New Yorkers recoup damages from any trespassing Brits. "It was immensely popular, having virtually unanimous approval of the citizenry, and yet it flouted fundamental principles of law," explains historian Forrest McDonald.

Here's the problem with the Trespass Act: it clashed with the 1783 peace treaty with England. Hamilton made a revolutionary legal argument that would become, in time, a bedrock of judicial review—that *federal law should trump state law*.

During the war, the Brits—even though New Yorkers hated them—were actually, well, operating under the laws of war. Those laws trump state laws. (Hamilton's sneaky agenda? He had a long game: legal precedents like this help solidify the union; they help us "Think Continentally.")

Hamilton's oral arguments "soared far above all competition" according to one contemporary, and the audience "listened with admiration for his impassioned eloquence." The judges were convinced by his logic, slashing the damages from £8,000 to £800.

The young lawyer fought for his convictions, but this made him a villain to some, as he helped the biggest "scoundrels in the universe." Yet it positioned Hamilton as a legal star, it gave him a pipeline of wealthy Tory clients, and he would juggle forty-five Tory cases in the coming years, giving him an income for his growing family.

It can pay to stick to your principles.

BEWARE SPECULATION

—

*"I do not know what effect the imprudent
speculations in Bank Script may produce."*

ICTURE NEW YORK AT the end of the Revolutionary War.
Nearly all the shops, homes, and taverns were clumped
below present-day Houston Street. There wasn't really
an "uptown" or a "midtown," as the island was still
covered with forests. Pigs still walked the streets. For seven brutal
years, the British had owned the island.

Then, on November 25, 1783, Evacuation Day—a holiday celebrated for the next 133 years—the redcoats slouched back to
King George, ushering in a new era that brimmed with promise.
New York would serve as the new nation's capital. The mood was
euphoric.

Amid this giddy backdrop, Hamilton grew his legal practice,
dashed off more political pamphlets, served as a tax collector,
and even, briefly, served as a congressman. He also found time for
every New Yorker's favorite hobby: obsessing over New York real
estate. At the time, buying land was the only real way to invest
your money; there was no stock market, no NASDAQ, no March
Madness office pool.

So he speculated. Nearly all the Founding Fathers did. Was it better to invest in the city, or maybe to buy some land upstate? One night Hamilton, his friend John Jay, and others discussed the issue at a dinner party, no doubt aided by several bottles of wine.

John Jay invested in downtown New York City. Smart move—it made him rich. Hamilton? As his son woefully reports, Hamilton "took the opposite view and invested in the lands of the northern counties of the state." So is that . . . good? "The wild lands were purchased at a few cents an acre, but they were not settled very rapidly."

Not settled very rapidly. That's a polite way of putting it. Hamilton could have invested in the Financial District—you know, the place with the skyscrapers—and instead he tossed the dice on some upstate wilderness. It's baffling. At nearly every turn of his career, Hamilton played chess when others played checkers. Not this time.

It was a curious bad bet, but from his gamble we can glean a larger lesson: beware speculation when you have a safer option. Someone gives you a sexy stock tip? Caveat emptor. Or, put differently, it's difficult to "beat the market." Even for financial geniuses like Alexander Hamilton.

FIND TIME FOR
THE QUILLS AND THE BILLS

—

"A nation cannot long exist without revenues."

1 787. THE NATION'S FUTURE LOOKED GRIM. There wasn't really much of a "United States" to speak of, as the only thing the states were "united" in, really, was toppling King George. Once that happened, they drifted apart.

Problem #1: The government couldn't pay the army.
Problem #2: There wasn't a government.

Thanks to years of fireworks and apple pie, we look back at July 4, 1776, as the birth of our nation, but this tradition forgets that the next decade, basically, was something of a hot mess. As Hamilton bemoaned, "We have neither troops nor treasury nor government."

Soldiers rioted. Debt grew. Chaos reigned.

Desperate for a stronger government that could actually get things done, Hamilton suggested the Constitutional Convention. And when the Constitution was written? It needed ratification. This was no foregone conclusion: Virginia and New York—the two biggest players—were swing states, as they both dreaded a strong central government. From France, Thomas Jefferson read the Constitution carefully and concluded, "There are very good articles in it and very bad. I do not know which predominate."

So Hamilton hatched an idea for a PR campaign: *The Federalist Papers*, or originally, simply *The Federalist*. It's hard to overstate their importance. Without them, New York and Virginia might not have joined the new nation. Without Virginia, there would be no George Washington as President.

Hamilton's original plan was to write a total of twenty essays, or "at the most 25," with the work divvied up among James Madison, John Jay, William Duer, Gouverneur Morris, and himself. It didn't quite shake out that way. Morris said he was too busy, Duer's essays didn't make the cut, and John Jay got sick (rheumatism) and eked out only five. Madison penned twenty-nine.

Hamilton? Fifty-one.

Writing as "Publius," he banged out these fifty-one essays in just a few short months. They were widely read and swayed popular opinion, and, it could be argued, they saved the nation from the maw of anarchy. Would the Constitution have been ratified without them? We'll never know.

So if you're Alexander Hamilton and you need to write these fifty-one essays that will change the course of history, how, exactly, do you do it? Maybe bunker yourself in a library? Furiously write all day in a coffee shop? Go on some writer's retreat in upstate New York?

No. That's not what you do. If you're Alexander Hamilton, you write these *while also working as a full-time lawyer.*

Let's let that sink in. He didn't even take a break from his law practice. How could he? The man had bills. Unlike the other

Founding Fathers, Hamilton didn't come from money or have the luxury of leisure.

Hamilton had Eliza and his baby boy Philip to feed, so every morning he commuted to his law office, wrote briefs, and argued before juries. Then, at night, instead of kicking back and binging on Netflix, he dashed off one of our nation's iconic documents.

And next time you're bored on an airplane? Consider this: Hamilton outlined the entire project while traveling. On a boat. As Eliza wrote years later, "My beloved husband wrote the outline of his papers in *The Federalist* on board one of the North River sloops while on the way to Albany . . . Public business so filled up his time that he was compelled to do much of his studying and writing while traveling."

Takeaway: If you're hungry and you have a burning passion, it is not necessary to quit your day job. You can do both. With the right schedule, the right mindset, and the right hustle, you can feed your creativity and keep paying the bills. Hamilton argued that "a nation cannot exist without revenues," and the same, surely, applies to your own household.

Too often we use our jobs as an excuse. "Oh, I'd love to write a screenplay," we say. "But I just don't have the time." Or it flips the other way: Creative types think that in order to be "true artists," they must sever ties with the corporate world and scrape by on peanuts. They think that a day job makes them a "sellout" or somehow less "pure." It's a false choice. You can be brilliant and also keep your health benefits. You can be an artist without being a starving artist. There's always more time than you think. It can be done. Just ask Hamilton.

HAMILTON THE MONARCHIST?

Back in 1780, years before anyone else had given the matter much thought, Hamilton asked Congress to "call immediately a convention of all the states" to draft a new Constitution. Now, in 1787, the rest of the world caught up.

Yet in a cruel twist, Hamilton had little clout at the Convention itself. Each state had to vote as one solid block. Hamilton's fellow New York delegates, appointed by the anti-Constitution governor, refused to play ball. Hamilton was muzzled. James Madison stole the show, taking minutes and wrangling the votes and brokering compromise after compromise. Madison is called the Father of the Constitution for good reason.

At some point, though, Hamilton stood up to give a speech.

It lasted for *six hours*. Oblivious to how bad it made him look, Hamilton proposed an "elected monarch" that would serve for life upon "good behavior." In fairness to him, the speech might have been a negotiation tactic (making the eventual compromise look more palatable), and the concept of "elected monarch" (as opposed to hereditary) was one others had also mulled over. Some delegates floated even goofier ideas, like a three-man presidency, sort of like a Roman triumvirate, that carved up the nation into geographic thirds.

Finally, Hamilton sat down. Many in the room were stunned. *Who was this guy? What was he thinking?*

Hamilton couldn't help it. The man spoke his mind. He did it when it helped him, he did it when it hurt him. One delegate called the speech "the most able and impressive he had ever heard." Yet it would haunt him.

The first clouds had just darkened Hamilton's sunny future. His enemies began to whisper.

CONQUER THE CREDIT

—

*" 'Tis by introducing order into our finances; by
restoring public credit not by gaining battles,
that we are finally to gain our object."*

DO YOU KNOW YOUR CREDIT SCORE? This is what happens when
it's too low:

- You're stuck with high interest rates on credit cards.
- You can't get a car loan.
- You can't get a mortgage.
- You might rack up more debt . . . which means more debt . . .
  which means more debt.

Bad credit can lead to bankruptcy, eviction, divorce, hair loss,
and basically the ruining of your life. (Don't worry, this gets less
depressing!) Now imagine what happens when the *entire economy* has no credit.

That brings us to April 30, 1789, when the United States had
a credit score that hovered somewhere between 0 and 0. On that
day, George Washington put his fidgety hand on the Bible and
swore the oath of office. "This great man," observed one onlooker, "was agitated and embarrassed more than he ever was by
the leveled cannon or pointed musket."

Hamilton was nervous, too. He had crunched the numbers and done the math: the nation was broke. The Revolutionary War had racked up a tab of $54,124,464.56 in federal debt. (Yes, he did his math to the penny.)

Here are just some of the many problems the nation faced:

- The army still hadn't been paid.
- The army threatened mutiny.
- No other country would loan the US money—too risky.
- No one else would *invest* in the US—too risky.
- Many states were going bankrupt.
- When the states *did* try and collect revenue, it backfired and people took up guns to rebel. (See: Shays' Rebellion.)

Think about it this way: What do you do if you are broke and you really, really need some cash?

You get a loan.

But where do you get that loan?

Friends, family, or contacts.

And what if they're all broke, too?

You go to the bank?

Yet the nation didn't have a bank. Back then, the word "capitalism" did not yet exist. If you wanted a loan to start your own business, then you asked your wealthy uncle. Oh, you didn't have a wealthy uncle? Tough. Then you planted cabbages.

Hamilton had a plan to change this.

Congress swore him in as the first treasury secretary on Friday, September 11, 1789. On Saturday he booked an emergency loan—to pay off immediate bills, basically—that helped save the nation from default. On Sunday he went fishing.

Kidding; this is Alexander Hamilton. On Sunday he began staffing up the treasury department. Soon it would dwarf every other government agency and he'd become the second most powerful man in the nation, trailing only George Washington.

Once again Hamilton moved quick—just like stealing cannons from the British. "Washington had no desire to lead Congress," explains Flexner. "This left a power vacuum into which Hamilton leaped, setting up, before Jefferson realized the possibility, his own bloc in Congress that became the Federalist Party. For a while, Hamilton led Congress."

You get the sense that Hamilton was put on the planet for this very moment. No precedent bound him. He could finally unleash all the plans, theories, and financial models that he had doodled in his army journal. As one historian put it, Hamilton was an "administrative genius" who "assumed an influence in Washington's cabinet which is unmatched in the annals of the American cabinet system."

Congress asked him for a report that outlined the nation's finances. *No problemo.* He dashed off a 51-page manifesto: "Report on the Public Credit." He then had the dense report read aloud in Congress—this took *hours*—which left half of Congress confused and the other half (likely) falling asleep. To oversimplify things, Hamilton's plan had four key components:

(Stay with me here.)

1) Debt
2) Banks
3) Bonds
4) Taxes

We'll cover each of these (*really exciting*) topics in a bit. For now, though, the point is that Hamilton realized that without bold action, the nation risked a financial meltdown. (See also: Greece 2016.) But trouble loomed. It's one thing to announce a plan; it's another to jam it through Congress.

Enter Thomas Jefferson.

The Sage from Monticello had finally returned from France (where he had been serving as an ambassador), and he did not like this plan; he did not like it one bit. He found it too British, too corrupt, too banky, and too anti-farmer. Jefferson feared that if Hamilton's plan went through, it would swing too much power to the federal government, undercutting the very premise of the American Revolution, which, from his perspective, was a revolt *against* centralized authority. Ever the champion of farmers, Jefferson believed that "those who labor in the earth are the chosen people of God," although it's unclear if he's referring to the plantation owners or the slaves.

To summarize:

Thomas Jefferson hated the banks.
James Madison hated the banks.
James Monroe hated the banks.
John Adams hated the banks.

Bankers are "swindlers and thieves," according to Adams. "Our whole banking system I ever abhorred . . . I continue to abhor and shall die abhorring."

Hamilton had read all the economic treatises. His enemies had not. Hamilton had studied finance since he was twelve years old at the trading shop. His enemies had not.

He knew the nation needed to conquer the credit, and he would find a way.

WHAT'S FREE TODAY
WILL COST YOU TOMORROW

—

"With respect to the conduct of such men [financial administrators], suspicion is ever eagle-eyed and the most innocent things are apt to be misinterpreted."

HAMILTON HAD GOBS OF CHANCES to make himself rich, especially while trying to convince Congress to swallow his bold plan.

He never accepted a nickel. When offered a cushy insider deal on a real estate project? He didn't take it. No cash from lobbyists, no speaking fees from Goldman Sachs, no donations from the Super PACs. No freebies. A solid principle for anyone at any age in any context—what's free today will cost you tomorrow. He knew even the *appearance* of crookedness could be his undoing, as "suspicion is ever eagle-eyed."

Remember his rich father-in-law, Philip Schuyler? Hamilton never accepted a dime from him, either. All that joking to John Laurens about looking for a sugar mama, it turns out, was just that—joking. The man had his pride.

Hamilton embraced this principle early. At the close of the Revolutionary War, after years of risking his life and bleeding for his country, Hamilton, like thousands of soldiers, was owed a pension worth five years of salary. The rest of the army clamored for their back pay. Some threatened a mutiny. (Quick aside: When the scene nearly escalated to violence, Washington addressed the angry officers and read them a letter. But before he did, he reached for his eyeglasses. "Gentlemen," he said, "you will permit me to put on my spectacles, for I have not only grown gray but also blind in service to my country." The grown men were moved to tears; they called off the mutiny. Washington had skills.)

Hamilton did not clamor for his pension. Instead he *refused* it. Since he was then a member of Congress, he feared that accepting a pension would invoke a conflict of interest. Now, when he became treasury secretary, to err on the side of caution he suspended his legal practice, offering it to longtime friend Robert Troup. His buddy marveled at the "serious injury" of this financial sacrifice, as Hamilton's "fortune was very limited and his family was increasing."

Hamilton kept his honor clean. "A man of irreproachable integrity, Hamilton severed all outside sources of income while in office," observes Chernow, "something that neither Washington nor Jefferson nor Madison dared to do."

GIVE WITHOUT FANFARE

—

The bearer [of this letter] is a soldier's widow in great distress who wants to go to her friends in the Jerseys but has not the means. If you could find her a place in some public wagon going that way, you would do an act of charity.

I am Sir Yr. Obed ser.

A HAMILTON

EVEN WHEN HE WAS light in the wallet, and even when busy trying to establish a bank, Hamilton gave freely to his friends and those in need. He and Eliza took in orphans and doled out loans that they couldn't really afford. He did pro bono legal work, accepted lower rates from poorer clients, and once was paid only in a "barrel of hams." He didn't create a showy "Hamilton Foundation" that made him the star, but instead he worked behind the scenes.

Just ask a young artist named Ralph Earl, who painted a collection of charming landscapes, portraits, and Revolutionary War battles. Earl lost his money and found himself in debtors' prison. Hamilton swooped in to the rescue: as his son tells us, he asked Eliza to "go to the debtors' jail to sit for her portrait and she induced other ladies to do the same . . . By this means, the artist made a sufficient sum to pay his debts."

He loved these kinds of tiny gestures.

Hamilton's enemies—Jefferson, Adams, and now James Madison—liked to sketch him as the greedy friend of the banks, the enemy of the poor. (As recently as June 2016, an op-ed piece in the *New York Times* scolded Hamilton's "contemptuous attitude toward the lower classes.") If he were alive today, he could counter this with some basic facts about his own philanthropy, but he probably wouldn't. He gave when no one was looking.

Many years later, shortly before he died, one night he heard a knock on the door (as legend has it). He opened it to see an old friend who, heavily in debt, needed an emergency loan. Hamilton was short on funds himself, but he somehow cobbled together $10,000. The old friend was Aaron Burr.

DON'T SKIMP ON THE LIFE INSURANCE

—

"I am poorer than when I went into office."

T HE FATHER OF AMERICAN FINANCE—the man on the $10 bill—had rotten luck with his own finances. Chronically poor, Hamilton spent the bulk of his career as a public servant, which then, as now, paid less than the private sector. In 1790, the job of treasury secretary paid $3,000 a year (only about 10 percent of Washington's salary), or about $73,000 in today's dollars. It's not chump change, but he had to support a wife, children, the charity and the loans to friends, and the dinners and schmoozing that's expected of polite society.

Another factor to consider: the real financial genius in the family might be *Eliza* Hamilton. One friend wrote to Hamilton that Eliza has "as much merit as your treasurer as you have as treasurer of the wealth of the United States." (How much did Eliza secretly help Hamilton behind the scenes? How many brilliant ideas were actually hers?)

Many years later, when Hamilton retired from public service, he admitted, "I am poorer than when I went into office."

But he had a plan!

He would return to work as a lawyer. Just like the sixty-five-year-old who craves retirement but knows he must keep grinding, Hamilton vowed to "allot myself . . . five or six years of more work than will be pleasant."

This was a fine plan. And it should have worked. When he eventually left the cabinet, Hamilton was still a young man—not yet forty—and if he worked another ten years, twenty years, or maybe even thirty years, there's no question he would have raked in the plum lawyer money. His family would have security.

But he didn't count on one thing: a duel on the shores of New Jersey.

His death would leave Eliza in a bad way. Their home cost more than she could afford, she had no income, and she still had all the kids to feed. Her debt forced her to write a friend, "As I am nearly out of cash, I take the liberty to ask you to negotiate a loan of three hundred dollars." Still loyal to their fallen leader, a group of Federalists donated $80,000 to the Eliza estate in secret, to preserve the Hamilton family's dignity. (Amazingly, this secret was kept until 1937.)

There's a larger lesson here, and it goes well beyond the specific need for life insurance: *Think about a range of scenarios.* Hamilton, like so many of us, really only planned for one financial future: the one where he lived a long life and commanded a high income. Most of us operate with that kind of subconscious bias. We skimp on savings, we hope for the best, and we rarely think about the "what ifs?" in life.

What if we get sick?

What if we get laid off?

What if we get challenged to a duel?

Hamilton, like most of the Founding Fathers, did not make *saving* a priority. We can learn from their mistakes.

Thanks to the very instruments that Hamilton created, we can use 401(k)s, automatic savings plans, and yep, even life insurance to answer all those What Ifs. Looking for a good option? There was actually an Alexander Hamilton Life Insurance Company, but in one final insult to the Hamilton legacy, in the year 2000, the firm was acquired by the Jefferson-Pilot Financial Insurance Company. The two still battle from beyond the grave.

OWN THE DEBT,
DON'T LET THE DEBT OWN YOU

—

"A national debt if it is not excessive will be to us a national blessing; it will be a powerful cement to our union."

THESE DAYS, OF COURSE, the words "national debt" have connotations of evil; anyone who says "More debt!" sounds as bonkers as someone saying "More crime!" But debt can have merit. In the 1790s, Hamilton's grand plan called for the federal government to absorb the $25 million of wartime debt that was owed by the states, which, in turn, would make the states beholden to the federal government.

Let's pause here. *Federal absorption of state debt.* What the hell does that really mean? It sounds like something that people would have very, very passionate opinions about on Facebook . . . but not really understand. Sort of like gluten.

Here's how it works: During the Revolutionary War, most states couldn't afford to pay their soldiers. So they racked up debt. Some states had very little debt—like Virginia. Some states, though, had a crushing debt that looked hopeless—like Massachusetts.

Hamilton's plan called for the federal government to gobble

up *all* of the debt, which would "be a powerful cement to our union." This would give the government teeth. If the federal government was to own all the debt, suddenly it could swing a bigger stick. This would help transform the united states into The United States.

Hamilton tapped into human nature: If someone owes you money, you will care about her survival. "Hamilton knew that bondholders would feel a stake in preserving any government that owed them money. If the federal government, not the states, was owed the money, creditors would shift their main allegiance to the central government," explains Chernow. "Hamilton's interest was not in enriching creditors or cultivating the privileged class so much as insuring the government's stability and survival."

This "debt assumption" was the linchpin of Hamilton's plan. Just one tiny problem: The South hated it. Most of the debt was owed by the northern states, so the South felt little need to belly up to the bar. *Why should we pay for your sloppy finances?*

Hamilton had two rebuttals:

ARGUMENT #1: THE SINKING FUND

HAMILTON *NEVER* INTENDED THE DEBT TO be permanent. (Debt is like tequila, scrambled eggs, and pornography—it's best in moderation.) He viewed debt as a temporary Band-Aid that would be retired within fifteen years. "The creation of debt should always be accompanied by the means of extinguishment," he patiently explained.

This advice is timeless. Take debt for student loans. It makes a good deal of sense, but only if there's a realistic way to pay it off. (In other words: Student loans for law school? Good debt. Credit card loans to buy a bigger TV? Bad debt.) Hamilton wrote frequently of the dangers of too much debt, even busting out the All-Caps to say that too much debt "is perhaps the NATURAL DISEASE of all Governments."

Hamilton created a "sinking fund," meaning that the government would make automatic payments to the debt so that it would, in time, sink. This is the great-great-grandfather of devices like your 401(k) plan, where a certain percentage of the paycheck is automatically invested. (Nearly everything involving dollars, it seems, can be traced back to Hamilton.)

ARGUMENT #2: THE NORTH DID THE FIGHTING

THE SECOND KEY ARGUMENT: YES, MOST of the wartime debt was owed by the northern states. Fair. But then again, most of the war was fought in the North.

There's an even subtler point. "A lot of historians don't seem to understand this, but Hamilton's plan called for an accounting of all the debts that each state paid, and if they paid more than their fair share, they would get back a credit," says financial historian Richard Sylla. Hamilton tallied up the costs of the war that each state had incurred. Then he tallied up the contributions of each state. If Virginia paid more than its fair share, the state would effectively get a "refund." Almost no one understood this.

There was also, of course, a third, unspoken argument about the debt:

TABOO UNSPOKEN ARGUMENT #3: SLAVERY

THE SOUTH DIDN'T HAVE AS MUCH debt because the South had slaves.

Abolition was such a controversial topic, so explosive, that it was never on the table. This focused all the debate on Hamilton's debt. "It was a testimony to the political genius of Thomas Jefferson and James Madison that they diverted attention from the grisly realities of southern slavery by casting a lurid spotlight on Hamilton's system as the paramount embodiment of evil," explains Chernow.

So the divide between North and South deepened.

The point is this: Hamilton didn't have the votes, so the plan looked dead in the water. But maybe they could find a compromise? Perhaps over dinner and a bottle of wine?

5
STYLE & ETIQUETTE

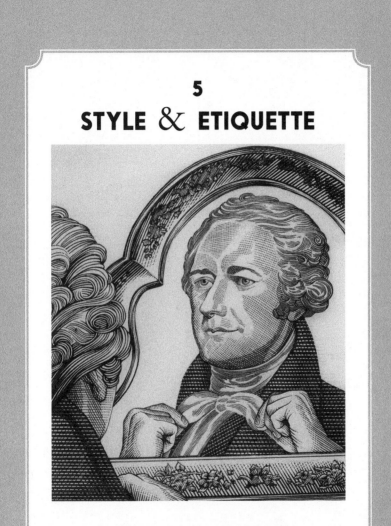

LOOK THE PART, ACT THE PART

LOOK THE PART, ACT THE PART

—

"A smart dress is essential."

HAMILTON WOULD HAVE SCOFFED at the saying "The clothes make the man." Guts make the man. Smarts make the man. Honor makes the man. Gods can wear rags, fools can wear silk.

Yet while style is not the *primary* measure of character, Hamilton believed that attire can serve a purpose. He knew, for example, that "a smart dress is essential" for boosting morale in the military because if, God forbid, a soldier lacked the right uniform, he would be "exposed to ridicule and humiliation." In other words: Look the part, act the part.

Hamilton took fashion seriously. While sweet-talking senators to create a bank, Hamilton would wear colors bright and bold: he was "dressed in a blue coat with bright buttons," remembers one dinner party guest, and "the skirts of his coat were unusually long. He wore a white waistcoat, black silk small clothes, white silk stockings."

And years later, when Hamilton created an army, he outlined the exact uniform that should be worn by General George Washington:

A blue coat without lapels, with lining collar and cuffs of buff, yellow buttons and gold epaulettes of double bullion tag with fringe, each having three stars. Collar cuffs and pocket flaps to have full embroidered edges.

Wait, but what should the general's hat look like?

A full cocked hat, with a yellow button gold loop, a black cockade with a gold eagle in the center and a white plume.

And the boots?

Long boots with stiff tops reaching to the center of the knee pan, the whole of black leather lined above with red morocco, so as just to appear . . .

How about a prop, something for a little flair?

A cut-and-thrust sword with a blade of not less than 28 nor more than 32 inches in length . . . its hilt of gold.

You can almost see Hamilton at his desk, doodling, trying out design after design, as if he's creating Washington's Bitmoji avatar.

Why did Hamilton care so much about nice threads? Armchair psychologists might suggest that since he came from the outer fringe of the West Indies, he wore flashy clothes to overcompensate. To this we should say . . . so what? The truth is that Hamilton *wasn't* from the aristocracy, so he didn't have the luxury of being casual. (In contrast, when he became President, Thomas Jefferson made a big show of answering the White House door in pajamas and "yarn stockings and slippers," proving that he was a man of the people.)

Hamilton knew the value of perception. How you present yourself to the world will influence, however subtly, the way you are treated by the world. So present well.

CARRY YOURSELF WITH DIGNITY, NOT DISGUST

—

"I have reflected on the etiquette proper to
be observed by the President . . ."

THINK OF ALL THE traditions of the White House: The President gives a State of the Union, pardons a turkey on Thanksgiving, and reluctantly sends troops into the Middle East. In 1789 we had none of these. There was no playbook. How should a President act? What do we call them? What should they wear? The Constitution makes no mention of the cabinet, much less the presidential etiquette. "I walk on untrodden ground," Washington said, acutely aware that his every move would "hereafter be drawn into precedent." Or as Madison put it, "We are in a wilderness without a single footstep to guide us."

So Alexander Hamilton jumped into the void. In one of many examples of how he acted as de facto prime minister, not just treasury secretary, he took it upon himself to mold Washington's image. Not twenty-four hours after the President asked if he had any thoughts on the matter, Hamilton "reflected on the etiquette proper to be observed by the President," and wrote a four-page letter that offers, like always, some hyperspecific advice.

His overall theme is that "the dignity of the office should be supported." It's a fair point. If a leader wants to be taken seriously, the leader should act seriously. No kissing babies.

Hamilton's guide to presidential etiquette:

1. "Avoid extensive disgust."

SOLID ADVICE. Try to avoid scrunching up your face like you smell rotten eggs. The broader context here:

> *Care will be necessary to avoid extensive disgust or discontent. Men's minds are prepared for a pretty high tone in the demeanor of the Executive, but I doubt whether for so high a one as in the abstract might be desirable.*

Translation: It's cool to be aloof, but don't be a jerk.

2. "The President to have a levee day once a week for receiving visits."

A "LEVEE" WAS A FORMAL CEREMONY, modeled after the British aristocracy, that sounds dreadfully dull. The President should "remain half an hour, in which time he may converse cursorily on indifferent subjects . . . and at the end of that half hour disappear." Washington appeared at these things in a velvet coat and satin breeches. He never shook hands or touched anyone, but nodded grimly and made stern eye contact. He even wore a ceremonial sword in a scabbard, which, it must be said, is a look that demands a comeback.

3. "The President to accept no invitations, and to give formal entertainments only twice or four times a year."

WHAT DAYS SHOULD HE HOLD THESE PARTIES? Hamilton has specific dates in mind: "the day of the declaration of independence, and that of the inauguration of the President." His advice is still followed to this day.

4. Once a week, "give informal invitations to family dinners ... Not more than six or eight to be invited at a time."

BY "FAMILY DINNER," Hamilton didn't mean Eliza or Angelica or his beloved son, Philip. Family dinners are "to be confined essentially to members of the Legislature and other official characters." And if you're hoping for a leisurely chat with the commander in chief over a few glasses of wine, think again, as "[t]he President [is] never to remain long at table."

These must have been excruciating. "No cheering ray of convivial sunshine broke through the cloudy gloom of settled seriousness," complained one senator, who was lucky enough to be invited. "At every interval of eating and drinking, [Washington] played on the table with a fork and knife, like a drumstick."

Not everyone loved these rules. But you know who did? Just hours after receiving Hamilton's letter, Washington picked up his quill and scribbled:

Dear Sir:

I beg you to accept my unfeigned thanks for your friendly communication . . . The matter chosen for doing it is most agreeable to me. It is my wish to act right . . .

With sentiments of sincere esteem and regard,
I am, dear sir, your obed't serv't,

Geo. Washington.

It's easy to make light of all this, but the office of the President *does* carry a certain gravitas. And as most leaders eventually learn, at a certain point, you *do* have to erect some boundaries with your old chummy colleagues. Dignity matters.

And before we accuse Hamilton of being too over the top, for perspective, John Adams once suggested that Washington be addressed as "His Highness, the President of the United States of America and Protector of their Liberties," or HHPOTUSAPOL for short.

SPRINKLE IN THE CHARM

—

"I would wish to charm you in every sense . . ."

HAMILTON OOZED CHARM. "HE came across as a man's man and a woman's man, meaning that he could dominate a brandy-and-cigars discussion of politics, then move across the room and flirtatiously commend the ladies on their dress or jewelry," writes historian Joseph Ellis. "Men found him admirable, clubby, and disarmingly potent. Women found him irresistible." (This, of course, is a bit of an old-timey guess as to what women "found irresistible." Who knows what they really thought. Were women ever truly asked?) One dinner guest remembers: "At dinner, whenever he engaged in the conversation, every one listened attentively. His mode of speaking was deliberate and serious; and his voice exceedingly pleasant."

He lit up every dinner party, dropping knowledge and holding court—all with an eye to creating his bank and debt system. (The mission never paused.) One of the most eminent diplomats on the world stage, France's Talleyrand, praised Hamilton's "delightful manners," his "cheerfulness," "great sweetness," and concluded that he was "one of the finest men in America."

His top legal rival, Aaron Burr, possessed his own kind of personal charm . . . but possibly of a different sort. "Burr's charm, attentiveness, and promiscuity . . . his lack of principle—all flow from his character," writes Brookhiser. "He was like a new refrigerator—bright, cold, and empty." Ouch. But even Burr might have agreed, as he once described himself as "a grave, silent, strange sort of animal, inasmuch that we not know what to make of him."

Hamilton might occasionally be "grave," but never "silent." He charmed the beautiful Eliza, and he, in turn, was charmed. "I would wish to charm you in every sense," he wrote his wife. "I shall never be satisfied with giving you pleasure." Hamilton adored the word. He called Eliza "my charmer," "my charming beloved wife," and his "saucy little charmer."

To his friends he showed a softer side. One night a friend of his, Judge Kent, stayed in Hamilton's New York home. The judge was fighting a cold, so he went to bed early. Before falling asleep, he saw Hamilton tiptoe into his room and cover him with an extra blanket, like a doting father. Hamilton then told him softly, "Sleep warm, little judge, and get well. What should we do if anything should happen to you?" It's, well, charming.

SEAL THE DEAL OVER DINNER

—

"We shall be happy to see you at dinner."

Hamilton loved his dinner parties. In the Revolutionary era, most dinners "lasted up to six hours—two hours longer than the average day at Congress," explains historian Joanne Freeman. "Usually they featured several courses, a generous selection of wines, and, after the tablecloth had been removed, a lengthy period during which the ladies enjoyed tea in the parlor and the men drank port, smoked cigars, ate fruit and nuts, and talked politics in the dining room."

Hamilton used dinners for both work and play. "I wish to have the advantage of a conversation with you," he wrote to a senator whose vote he needed. "If you will name a day for taking a family dinner with me . . . The chief subjects will be additional *funds* for public Debt and the *Bank*." Sounds like one hell of a party.

Not everyone loved the Hammie Show. John Adams scowled that Hamilton was an "insolent coxcomb who rarely dined in good company where there was good wine without getting silly and vaporing about his administration, like a young girl about her brilliants and trinkets."

Dinners let you look someone in the whites of their eyes and make a personal connection. They let you seal the deal. Email is efficient and phone calls are inevitable, but when you're wooing a client and the stakes are high, sometimes you need to splurge on the lobster.

The stakes could not have been higher in 1790. Hamilton had unleashed his minions—one senator called them his "Gladiators"—to scrounge up votes in Congress. He led the first great vote-mustering effort in the nation's history, a campaign that brings to mind LBJ's wrangling for the Civil Rights Act or Lincoln's push to pass the Thirteenth Amendment.

Gridlock crippled the government. (Sound familiar?) "Congress met and adjourned from day to day without doing anything," Jefferson remembered, "the parties being too much out of temper to do business together." Two debates consumed the government offices on 57 Maiden Lane:

1) Should the federal government assume state debts?
2) Where should the capital reside?

Hamilton insisted that the capital should remain exactly where it was: his hometown New York, as "this city is the best station for that honorable body." This made Jefferson queasy. He viewed the city as a hotbed of corruption, bankers, and sin. (In other words, "New York Values.") Jefferson and Madison, of course, pushed for a capital in their beloved Virginia.

Hamilton was in a jam. If he failed to consolidate the state debt, his entire financial system would crumble. "Every part of it has the nicest sympathy with every other part," he explained. "Wound one limb and the whole tree shrinks and decays."

He lacked the votes. But maybe he could broker a deal over dinner?

The official account of the most celebrated dinner party in American history comes from Jefferson, who allegedly saw Hamilton pacing outside Washington's home, distracted and down in the dumps. "His look was somber, haggard, and dejected," Jefferson recalled. "Even his dress [was] uncouth and neglected," which was very un-Hamiltonian.

"What on earth is the matter?" Jefferson supposedly asked Hamilton, or something of the sort.

Hamilton complained that his plan had no chance of getting through Congress.

"I'm really a stranger to the subject," replied Jefferson in one whopper of a lie. (In fact, more recent research casts some doubt on this entire episode, but we'll roll with the traditional telling.)

Jefferson, always happy to lend Hamilton a helping hand, suggested that they have dinner with his pal James Madison. Perhaps cooler heads would prevail? "It was observed," Jefferson remembered, "that as the pill [assumption of debt] would be a bitter one to the southern states, something should be done to soothe them."

They discussed the matter over food, wine, and candlelight. No one else was in the room where it happened, but we do know that hours later, after presumably more wine, the nation's capital would be in the swamps of the Potomac, and the federal government would assume the $25 million of state debt, an infusion of power that could never be undone.

There is little question that Hamilton won. The proof lies with Jefferson himself, who later tried to backtrack from his role at the Grand Dinner Bargain, also known as the Compromise of 1790. "I was duped into it by the Secretary of the Treasury," he complained, "then insufficiently understood by me, and of all the errors of my political life this has occasioned me the deepest regret."

One senator bemoaned Hamilton's masterful manipulation of power: "Everything . . . is prearranged by Hamilton."

His victory was not yet complete. He still needed his bank. But the kid from the West Indies, somehow, now perched atop the political establishment. There were some in Manhattan who even proposed a new name for New York City: "Hamiltoniana."

GROOM WITH GUSTO

—

"Flour is very necessary as an ingredient in the soup of the troops and for the purpose of dressing their hair."

GROOMING IS IMPORTANT. A clean shave, for example, embodies much of what Hamilton holds dear: the triumph of order over chaos, the mastery of one's environment, the taming of one's destiny. Every portrait shows Hamilton with a smooth jaw and not a speck of hair out of place. A morning shave gives confidence, control, clarity.

"John Wood shaved and dressed me in New York," Hamilton once observed to a friend. "I have found him sober and punctual and he has done my business to my satisfaction." (Always a plus when your barber is sober.)

Hamilton had his hair styled *daily.* "I recollect being in my father's office in New York when he was under the hands of his hair-dresser (which was his daily course)," remembers his son. On the back of the head, the "hair was long. It was plaited, clubbed up, and tied with a black ribbon. His front hair was [pomaded], powdered, and combed up and back from his forehead."

What, exactly, did the Founding Fathers use as hair product?

Flour. When in charge of the army, Hamilton observed that "a proportion of flour is very necessary as an ingredient in the soup of the troops and for the purpose of dressing their hair." (It's unclear what's more unpleasant: soup that's used as hair product, or hair product that's used in soup.)

Good grooming instills discipline. Remember that essay that Hamilton wrote, as a college kid, called "The Farmer Refuted"? It's the full-throated cry for revolution that put him on the map. In it he imagines a doomsday scenario where America bows to the King. "If Great-Britain can order us to come to her," Hamilton warns with foreboding, then "we are as abject slaves . . . with uncombed hair."

CLOSE WITH A FLOURISH

—

"The jury will mark every muscle of his
face, every motion of his eye . . ."

ET'S BRIEFLY JUMP FORWARD a few years. On a cold winter night in 1799, in downtown Manhattan, a young woman went missing. She was engaged to be married. The night she disappeared, her fiancé looked "white as ashes and trembled all over like a leaf," according to one witness, and two weeks later, the woman's dead body was found, fully clothed, at the bottom of a well. The city charged the fiancé with murder. His name was Levi Weeks.

New York went bananas. The Manhattan Well Murder trial soon became the O. J. Simpson trial of the eighteenth century, the nation's first blockbuster murder mystery. The trial had it all: a pretty young woman, a whodunit, a great villain in Levi Weeks, drug use, betrayal, a possible rape. As the official indictment charged, the accused lacked "the fear of God before his eyes," and instead was "moved and seduced by the instigation of the devil." The woman's family kept the body in an open coffin for three days, and then, perhaps to stoke the city's lust for vengeance, they even displayed the rotting corpse on a public street.

The trial also featured two lawyers who teamed up to defend the accused—Alexander Hamilton and Aaron Burr.

The tiny legal community of 1790s New York can seem a bit incestuous, with counsels working together one week, then dueling the next. Hamilton and Burr had joined forces before. "Hamilton cut the more airy figure, pirouetting about the courtroom with that dancer's body, beautifully clothed, gesturing gracefully, ever eloquent, and seemingly inexhaustible," explains Sedgwick. "His rhetorical elevation wasn't just to convey superiority (although it did have that effect) but to take the long view. To Hamilton, a case was about the principle of the case." Burr? He was craftier. More cunning.

New Yorkers swarmed the courthouse to see the two of them side by side, arguing the Trial of the Century. The court had to turn onlookers away, as the mob outside chanted, "Crucify him! Crucify him!"

Hamilton never cared much for mobs, and he chided the city for making a spectacle of the violence: "Why has the body been exposed for days in the public streets in a manner the most indecent and shocking?"

Then he got to work. In just a few quick days, Hamilton and Burr whipped together a defense that had a solid alibi, medical experts, and reports from coroners that foreshadowed *CSI*. Their sleuthing uncovered a second, more likely suspect for murder, Richard Croucher, who was a "shady salesman of ladies' garments."

Hamilton built his case brick by brick, point by point, one fact leading to the next. And then came the flourish. When Hamilton grilled Croucher on the witness stand, as legend has it, he dramatically held a candle next to the man's face, making him glow like the devil. "The jury will mark every muscle of his face, every motion of his eye," Hamilton said, staring at the sinister glow. He implored the jury to "look through that man's countenance to his conscience."

According to some, Croucher confessed on the spot. According to others, Hamilton felt so confident that he waived his right to a closing argument—possibly the first time in his life he declined to speak—and the jury took only five minutes to deliberate. Team Hamilton-Burr won.

To add one coda to the eternal Hamilton-Burr rivalry, by still another account, it was actually Aaron Burr who held the candle, dramatically announcing, "Behold the murderer, gentlemen!" Maybe Burr held the candle. Maybe Hamilton held the candle. Regardless, we know that Hamilton was a showman who loved his courtroom theatrics. Logic can have style. And in just a few short years, the two men would once again collaborate, on the shores of Weehawken, New Jersey, to close Hamilton's life with a flourish.

RELISH THE ARTS

—

[Regarding a man he admired]: "He possessed a pretty taste for the fine arts, and had himself attained some proficiency in poetry, music and painting."

A TRUE LADY OR GENTLEMAN, of course, should not neglect the arts. From Hamilton's grandson, we know that he "had a love of the fine arts and was something of a print collector and an amateur painter, for it appears he advised Mrs. Washington in regard to the paintings she bought." It's touching to imagine Hamilton, after spending all day working on his bank, then accompanying Martha Washington to the art gallery.

The Hamiltons also went to the theater, took in the opera, and decorated their home with prints, woodwork, and copper line engravings. "I know Hamilton likes the beautiful in every way," Angelica told Eliza. "The beauties of nature and of art are not lost on him."

He could sing, he could play the piano, and he played the harp with his daughter. He loved to sing so much, in fact, that at one dinner party, many years later, he leaped up on the table and belted out a song:

'Twas in the merry month of May
When bees from flower to flower did hum,
Soldiers through the town marched gay,
The village flew to the sound of the drum.

. . .

We're going to war, and when we die
We'll want a man of God nearby,
So bring your Bible and follow the drum.

The takeaway: Even though Hamilton is known as a man of *finance,* he knew the import of cultivating the mind in ways more supple than numbers, words, or logic. The overworked treasury secretary could have focused only on his job, but he didn't. What good is a brain without a soul?

THE ORIGINAL DREAM TEAM

The '92 Olympic basketball team of Michael Jordan, Magic Johnson, and Larry Bird is referred to as the original "Dream Team." False. That honor goes to the first roster of the United States' government. It's packed with all-stars:

STARTING 5:

President: George Washington
Vice President: John Adams
Secretary of the Treasury: Alexander Hamilton
Secretary of State: Thomas Jefferson
De facto Chief of Staff: Alexander Hamilton (Yes, he played two positions.)

BENCH:

(6th Man of the Year): Chief Justice: John Jay
Speaker of the House: James Madison
Secretary of War: Henry Knox—Washington's old artillery captain, and one of Hamilton's early backers.
Minister to France: James Monroe
Attorney General: Edmund Randolph (the Christian Laettner of the team. And if you don't remember who Christian Laettner is, well, exactly.)

(HONORARY) COACH:

Benjamin Franklin, who died one year into Washington's first administration, at the age of eighty-four. In one bleak moment at the Constitutional Convention, Franklin suggested that they join together in prayer. According to legend, Hamilton joked that they didn't need any "foreign aid."

MAKE TIME FOR MISCHIEF

—

"To do mischief he must work in the dark."

OUR MAN WASN'T EXACTLY what you'd call a "prankster." (As great-great-great-great-great-grandson Douglas Hamilton says, "Honestly, I think he was a pretty serious guy.") But he did flash the occasional burst of playfulness.

At the Constitutional Convention, Hamilton supposedly made a bet with his friend Gouverneur Morris. This is the man who inked the words "We, the People," and then, years later, would deliver the eulogy at Hamilton's funeral.

Hamilton gave Morris a dare. Everyone knew that George Washington, who always carried himself with great dignity, kept some physical distance between him and everyone else. Some said he had a "natural coldness." The general didn't like to be touched.

So Hamilton egged Morris on, daring him to give Washington a friendly slap on the back. Morris accepted. As Chernow tells the story, "Morris found Washington standing by the fireplace in a drawing room and genially cuffed him on the shoulder: 'My dear general, how happy I am to see you look so well.' Washington fixed Morris with such a frigid gaze that Morris was sorry that he had ever taken up Hamilton's dare."

The takeaway? The next time someone busts your chops for goofing around, remind them that even in the vortex of the Constitutional Convention—the very inception of the nation—there's always time for mischief.

PARLEZ FRANÇAIS

—

"I was very glad to learn, my dear daughter, that you were going to begin the study of the French language."

Accarding to Hamilton, a person of merit should speak more than one language, and ideally that language should be French. He studied the language as a boy on Nevis; he continued those lessons in college, and years later, deep into his career, he hired a tutor for some extra gloss. He even subscribed to French newspapers, his thirst for information not slaked by just one language.

"Although he had never been in Europe, he spoke our language like a Frenchman," admired Madame de la Tour du Pin, a French aristocrat who emigrated to America. Hamilton also studied Greek and Latin in college, and his grandson notes that "it has been stated that in his earliest infancy he was able to read the Hebrew Decalogue."

Knowing a second language can help you in surprising ways. Hamilton's French helped him with the ladies, it helped charm his father-in-law (Philip Schuyler also spoke French), it wooed the upper crust, and it shored up gaps from his humble beginnings. It even helped win the Revolutionary War.

Surely Hamilton and Lafayette would not have been so close if the former had not spoken French, and it was Hamilton who urged Lafayette to request military aid from King Louis XVI. Without Lafayette we might not have won the war; without Hamilton we might not have had Lafayette.

Hamilton's French also helped train the army. Early in the war, when the army was still a tattered mess with no discipline, Washington invited a German military expert, the fantastically named Baron Frederick William Augustus von Steuben, who had served under Frederick the Great, to come train the troops.

Only one problem: von Steuben spoke very little English. He did, however, speak French. Washington didn't. Hamilton did. Von Steuben took over as provisional Inspector General of the army, "strutting around Valley Forge, teaching the amateur troops to march in formation, load muskets, and fix bayonets and sprinkling his orders with colorful goddamns and plentiful polyglot expletives that endeared him to the troops," as Chernow tells it. Von Steuben and Hamilton "became fast friends, united by French and their fondness for military lore and service." Von Steuben even wrote a new training manual for the army, but he wrote it in French. Good thing the army had a translator.

BE COURTEOUS, SIR

———

"I remain your obedient servant."

COURTESY COUNTS. IT DOESN'T MATTER if you're talking to a friend, coworker, boss, date, lover, or someone threatening to shoot you with a pistol—always be polite.

Hamilton, like all the Founding Fathers, was cartoonishly courteous. Every letter drips with respect. Even the briefest and most functional of missives—the equivalent of a one-line email, or maybe a text—come festooned with pleasantries. Consider this note from Hamilton to Jefferson on June 26, 1792:

> *Mr. Hamilton presents his respectful compliments to Mr. Jefferson & requests to be favoured with a copy of his Report concerning the distillation of Fresh from Salt-Water.*

When's the last time you "presented your respectful compliments" when you asked for an invoice?

Hamilton and Jefferson remained cordial as enemies. Later, when tensions flared between France and Britain, and when the two men butchered each other in the press, Hamilton still began his letters with courtesies such as "The Secretary of the Treasury presents his Respects to The Secretary of State." (The Founders do a lot of writing in the third person.) Hamilton signs off with one of the era's go-to salutations: "I have the Honor to be with great respect sir Your Most Obedient servant."

The most delicious example of the courtesy-at-all-cost, of course, is the flurry of letters that led to Hamilton's eventual duel. When Burr kicked off the dueling protocol, he threw down the gauntlet with this smackdown: "Thus, Sir, you have invited the course I am about to pursue." *Boom!* After using coded language to threaten to kill the man, Burr signs the letter, "I have the honor to be Your Ob st." (Even the abbreviations are adorable; the Founders truncated things like "Your Obedient Servant" to "Your Ob st." just as we use shortcuts like "ttyl" or "thx" or "wtf.")

Courtesy is a lost art. Our politicians call each other names, we send angry emails laced with sarcasm, and we snipe at each other in traffic and on Twitter. How much energy do we waste on venom? So the next time you get in a fender bender and it's the other guy's fault, first address him as "My Dear Sir." And if things escalate and you have to call the cops, remind him that you remain, as always, his obedient servant.

6
LEISURE

[HAMILTON HAD NOTHING to say about leisure.]

7
FRIENDS & FAMILY

PUT THE FATHER IN FOUNDING FATHER

PUT THE FATHER IN FOUNDING FATHER

—

"Experience more and more convinces me that
true happiness is only to be found in the
bosom of one's own family."

IN THE EARLY 1790S, fresh off his Debt Assumption victory, Hamilton looked toward the next step in his master plan: creating the US bank. Yet he and Eliza seemingly had another master plan: raising as many children as humanly possible. The Hamiltons were prolific at everything they did, and that includes baby-making: they had *eight* kids.

Let's look back to the birth of his first child, Philip, in 1782. The new father playfully wrote a friend to describe his new baby:

He is truly a very fine young gentleman, the most agreeable in his conversation and manners of any I ever knew . . . he is handsome, his features are good . . . and he has a method of waving his hand that announces the future orator.

But what does the baby look like?

He stands however rather awkwardly and his legs have
not at all the delicate slimness of his father's. It is feared he
may never excel as much in dancing which is probably the
only accomplishment in which he will not be a model. If he
has any fault in manners, he laughs too much. He has now
passed his seventh month.

Clichés like "Family First" are all too common, but with Hamilton this seems to really be the case. It's telling that in the above letter, only *after* the news about his son does he add, as a throwaway line, "I had almost forgotten to tell you, that I have been pretty unanimously elected by the legislature of this state, a member of Congress."

Philip soon became the "flower of the family," according to one grandson, and he seemed destined to follow the old man's footsteps. Yet Hamilton doted on all the kids. Eliza almost certainly deserves more of the credit here, but Hamilton taught the kids French, sang with them, helped them with studies, read them the Bible. As one of the children later described:

I distinctly recollect the scene at breakfast in the front
room of the house in Broadway. My dear mother, seated
as was her wont, at the head of the table with a napkin in
her lap, cutting slices of bread and spreading them with
butter for the younger boys, who, standing at her side, read
in turn a chapter in the Bible or a portion of Goldsmith's
"Rome." When the lessons were finished the father and the

elder children were called to breakfast, after which the boys were packed off to school.

It's a good reality-check. Whatever job you have, no matter how worthy, it's unlikely to be as important as the founding of America. Yet Hamilton knew that the infant nation was never as important as the actual infants.

POUR A SECOND GLASS

—

"[I request] a dozen wine glasses . . . two
ale-glasses . . . two tumblers."

T HERE'S ALWAYS TIME FOR a drink with friends. A few
months after Philip was born, when Hamilton first
moved into his new home at 57 Wall Street, he requested these items immediately:

- *four pint decanters if to be had, if not two quart*
- *a dozen wine glasses*
- *two ale-glasses to hold about a pint each*
- *two tumblers.*

"You will oblige me by procuring these articles as soon as
possible, having them carefully packed up in a small box," he in-
structs, adding that they should be immediately sent "as soon as
they arrive by water . . . I shall not be able to give a friend a glass
of wine 'till these arrive, for they are not to be had here. Let me
know what they cost by the first opportunity." Just how critical
are the wineglasses? He orders them without even knowing the
cost!

Let's remember that other maxim of his: "It is a maxim of my life to enjoy the present good with the highest relish, and to soften the present evil by a hope of future good." Surely that can involve a second glass of wine.

To be clear: Hamilton was no drunkard. Take a scene from the Revolutionary War. When negotiating a prisoner exchange, he broke bread with some British officers at the dinner table. He found that the Brits "do their best to be agreeable," but also had the habit of "swallowing a large quantity of wine every day, and in this I am so unfortunate that I shall make no sort of figure with them." Hamilton drank socially, not to get drunk. Getting drunk means losing control, and Hamilton never lost control. (At least not when he was wearing pants. More on that in a bit . . .)

FRIENDS BEFORE POLITICS

—

"My friendship for you will survive all revolutions."
—HAMILTON TO LAFAYETTE,
DURING THE FRENCH REVOLUTION

H AMILTON ISN'T THE KIND of guy who befriends you in college, moves to a different city, stops texting, can't attend your wedding, and then only "likes" the occasional post on Facebook. He's a friend for life. Even if you disagree with him politically.

Consider some of Hamilton's friends from his college days at King's College: Hercules Mulligan, Robert Troup, and Edward Stevens. (Remember Edward Stevens, or "Neddy"? He goes all the way back to the St. Croix days.)

Now consider some of Hamilton's friends from his powerhouse days as treasury secretary: Hercules Mulligan, Robert Troup, and Edward Stevens.[*]

---

[*] Edward Stevens and Hamilton reunited at King's College, and when both were adults, a few people noted how similar they looked. *Very* similar. Could they be . . . brothers? Some historians have speculated that Hamilton was secretly an illegitimate Stevens, which would explain the Stevens family's generosity (they took Hamilton in as a kid). There have also been theories that Hamilton was part Jewish, or part black, or part Targaryen. The debate continues.

Hamilton was loyal to his friends and happy to support them however he could. He mentored Hercules Mulligan's child. He was of course "friendly" with his sister-in-law Angelica, who fretted that he worked too hard in pushing through his banking plan. "Our dear Hamilton writes too much and takes no exercise and grows too fat," Angelica complains to Eliza. (Even Founding Fathers, apparently, get body shamed.) "You will take care of his health and good looks. Why, I shall find him on my return a dull, heavy fellow!"

That was unlikely. No matter how busy, Hamilton squeezed in time for his buddies from the Revolutionary War. And he had every reason to think that his best friend, John Laurens, would remain his companion for life. After Yorktown, when the war was all but over, an exuberant Hamilton wrote to his friend:

Peace made, my dear friend, a new scene opens. The object then will be to make our independence a blessing. To do this, we must secure our <u>Union</u> on solid foundations, a herculean task.

The two of them would have been a formidable political duo—both brilliant, charismatic, and opponents of slavery. Laurens could have given Hamilton a powerful ally in South Carolina, a way to protect his southern flank. He could have also helped him establish his bank. Hamilton continues:

Quit your sword, my friend, put on the <u>toga</u>, come to Congress.

Alas, "toga" was not a reference to a toga party or a Roman orgy, but to the classical idea of how Roman soldiers fought in wars and then, after wielding the sword, retired to the Senate as elder, toga-wearing statesmen.

We know each other's sentiments; our views are the same;
we have fought side by side to make America free. Let us
hand in hand struggle to make her happy.

John Laurens never replied.

It's possible he never read the letter. Long after the Revolutionary War had *effectively* ended, but before the official peace treaty, Laurens, against orders, led his troops on a daring—and arguably pointless—ambush. He was shot and killed. Hamilton was crushed, writing to General Nathanael Greene (who knew Laurens during the war), "I feel the loss of a friend I truly and most tenderly loved, and one of a very small number."

Or take that third member of the Bromantic Triangle: the Marquis de Lafayette. Back in the winter of 1777, Hamilton and the Marquis had spent hours chatting about war, honor, politics, and romance. They stayed in touch and remained close. "It is a hard thing for me to be separated from the friends I love the best, and to think that our daily conversations are reduced to a few letters," Lafayette wrote from Paris.

Then, in the 1790s, came the French Revolution. Jefferson cheerfully praised the uprising, confident of its success, even predicting that within two years, France would have "a tolerably free constitution" without "having cost them a drop of blood." Oops.

(Later, when Jefferson realized that, actually, the French Revolution would get rather messy, he famously explained, "The tree of liberty must be refreshed from time to time with the blood of patriots and tyrants.")

Hamilton was more skeptical, thinking the savage violence "a disgrace." Yet even as he would later marshal the United States in a quasi-war with France, he still treasured his friendship with Lafayette. During the darkest days of Franco-American relationships, Hamilton writes, "[B]ut away with politics the rest of my letter shall be dedicated to assure you that my friendship for you will survive all revolutions."

Lafayette gave him a hug from across the Atlantic. "I hope you know that our former friendship has been in my heart unaltered, and that from the early times which have linked our brotherly union to the last moment of my life I shall ever be your affectionate friend."

We all have "that friend" who has some nutty political beliefs. Just as Hamilton and Lafayette could look past the French Revolution, we can ignore those cringe-worthy posts from "that friend" on Facebook. Friendship runs deeper than politics. (And okay, sure, maybe also click "Hide Posts from This User.")

KISS FREELY

—

"Kiss my boy a thousand times."

HAMILTON WAS A KISSER. He kissed his wife, his in-laws, his children. Affection flowed from his lips the way words gushed from his pen. Just some of the many, many kisses from Alexander Hamilton:

"I kiss your hand." —To Eliza

"Kiss my boy a thousand times. A thousand loves to yourself." —To Eliza, speaking of Philip (He loved offering kisses by the thousand.)

"Give my love to my darling Philip and kiss with all possible tenderness." —To Eliza

"Kiss your children for me." —To Angelica

"Kisses and blessings without number to you and my children." —To Eliza (The only thing better than a thousand kisses—infinite kisses!)

"Kiss Kitty for me and give my love to Angelica." —To Eliza

The kissing traces back to when he wrote this poem:

I had the waters gently glide,
And vainly hush'd the heedless wind,
Then, softly kneeling by her side,
I stole a silent kiss—

The larger point here? There's no need to be stingy with affection. It's easy to take our relationships for granted, to flinch from intimacy, and to put Love on something of a cruise control. Hamilton knew that just *caring* about someone isn't enough—you need to show it. Bonus? The very act of affection can help us feel more affectionate; as psychologists have shown in study after study, the act of smiling can make someone more likely to be happy. Just as books can fuel our knowledge, affection can fuel our love.

ADDITIONAL HAMILTONIAN AWESOMENESS

Hamilton did more by 9 a.m. than most people do all week. In addition to everything else in this book, some other random bits of Hamiltonian Awesomeness:

Founded the *New-York Evening Post*
Yep, Hamilton started the same *New York Post* that exists today. Over the years it would drop the "Evening" and add more puns (and a Page Six), but it remains the longest continuously operated daily paper in the nation.

Present during Benedict Arnold's treason
When Arnold was discovered as a British spy, Hamilton was in the room where it happened. He seemed to have a Forrest Gump–like quality of attending every key scene in the Revolution.

Established legal precedent that truth counts as a defense
Before the Supreme Court of the State of New York, he argued that a truthful statement cannot be defamatory. (You're welcome, TMZ.)

Wrote a draft of Haiti's constitution
In 1799, Hamilton dashed off some "thoughts that are very crude but perhaps they may afford some hints" about the government of Haiti. Those "crude thoughts" became the blueprints of Haiti's constitution.

Helped reopen King's College as Columbia
He finally got that honorary degree. (Given the timing of the Revolutionary War, Hamilton technically dropped out of college. Slacker.)

Sparked the idea for NASA

In 1778, while serving as an aide-de-camp, he wrote a letter to John Laurens suggesting "men of merit shall, before too long, aspire to the celestial domain. To furnish this objective, Congress must spur manufacturing, industry, and ingenuity. We must build a *winged vessel* that can reach the stars." Okay, I made all that up, but at this point, would it really surprise you?

KNOW THE BEST MEDICINE

—

"I hope you have been attentive to your medicine."

THE AVERAGE LIFE SPAN in the eighteenth century, according to some estimates, was in the forties to fifties. Blame infant mortality (a big problem), disease, and bullets from vice presidents. And then there was yellow fever. During yellow fever outbreaks, panicked city-dwellers would flee the crowds and head to the country.

No one was immune. In 1793, the dreaded yellow fever kissed the Hamilton children, Eliza, and Hamilton himself. Washington, alarmed by Hamilton's illness, sent him a note of concern and six bottles of wine. Thomas Jefferson, well, had quite a different reaction to Hammie's near-death experience.

When Jefferson heard that Hamilton was "ill," he accused him of playing hooky:

His family think him in danger and he puts himself so by his excessive alarm. He had been miserable several days before from a firm persuasion he should catch it.

But maybe that was too subtle? Jefferson elaborates on the fakery of Alexander Ferris Bueller:

*A man as timid as he is on the water, as timid on horseback,
as timid in sickness, would be a phenomenon if his courage, of which he has the reputation in military occasions,
were genuine.*

Hamilton has been accused of many things, but "timid" is especially rich. (This from Jefferson, who galloped away from the
British during the Revolutionary War.)

Hamilton recovered, as did the rest of the family. Yet they
would soon be tested again. When the oldest and favorite son,
Philip, was fifteen, he was "attacked with a severe, bilious fever,
which soon assumed a typhus character," explained the attending
physician.

Philip went comatose, and the doctor threw him in "hot baths
of Peruvian bark and rum." Hamilton was away on business
doing Hamiltonian things, but when he heard the news he raced
home to be with his boy, who he feared was dead. He must have
had flashbacks to St. Croix, all those years ago, when his mother
lay in the home's only bed, coughing, bleeding, dying.

The doctor picks up the story:

*In the course of the night . . . Hamilton arrived at his home
under the full expectation that his son was no more. But to
his great joy he still lived . . . He immediately came to my
room where I was sleeping, and although I was then personally unknown to him, awakened me and taking me by
the hand, his eyes suffused with tears of joy, he observed,
"My dear Sir, I could not remain in my own house without
first tendering to you my grateful acknowledgment for the*

valuable services you have rendered my family in the preservation of my child."

But Hamilton didn't remain a spectator. Like a concerned parent who spends hours on WebMD and then asks the doctor thoughtful questions, he did everything in his power to nurse Philip to health. Remember those classes he took at King's College? Hamilton had studied anatomy. And he forgot nothing. The doctor later recalled that Hamilton:

> *[d]evoted himself most assiduously to the care of his son, administering with his own hand every dose of medicine or cup of nourishment that was required. I may add that this was his custom in every important case of sickness that occurred in his family.*

Hamilton would do anything to keep his children safe. Anything, of course, except risk their honor. To be continued . . .

NEVER CHEAT

—

"I attended her into a room apart from the family . . ."

A ND NOW OUR STORY takes a darker turn. Hamilton, it turns out, was not a saint.

In 1791, Hamilton was thirty-four years old. One night he heard a knock at the door. He put down his work—presumably something to do with his banking plan. At the time he lived in Philadelphia, the nation's temporary capital, at the corner of Walnut and 3rd Street.

He opened the door and saw a woman. Young. Pretty. "Was it raining that night," wonders Sedgwick, "or does it only seem as though it was, since damp clothes, chilled skin, and dripping hair would do much to convey the sensual appeal of the beleaguered young woman."

She introduced herself as Maria Reynolds. *Can I speak to you alone?* she asked.

He quietly led her inside. "I attended her into a room apart from the family," Hamilton later admitted, knowing that Eliza and Philip and the other children were home. Perhaps they spoke in whispers. With tears in her eyes, Maria told him that her husband was abusive, dangerous, and that she needed his help.

"Sure, I'm happy to help," Hamilton said, and then he raised his voice to call inside. "Eliza? Honey? Can you come here? Maybe we can lend this woman some money."

Sadly, of course, Hamilton said nothing of the kind. His normal maxims would give crystal-clear direction: *Never cheat. Flirt . . . but don't cross the line. Always faithful. Hide nothing.*

He did none of those things. In perhaps the one great failing of his life, the next day, as Hamilton tells us:

I put a bank bill in my pocket and went to the house. I inquired for Mrs. Reynolds and was shown upstairs, at the head of which she met me and conducted me into a bedroom. I took the bill out of my pocket and gave it to her. Some conversation ensued from which it was quickly apparent that other than pecuniary consolation would be acceptable.

Let's pause to acknowledge that "other than pecuniary consolation" is the best euphemism in history for "sex." Soon they did it again. And again. And again. "I had frequent meetings with her, most of them at my own house," he confessed. *In Eliza's very bed.*

In a happy coincidence, Eliza and the kids had planned a trip to her father's mansion in Albany, leaving Hamilton home all alone for the summer. While she was gone—and while Hamilton was providing other than pecuniary consolation to Maria—he wrote his wife doting letters, inquiring as to her health. "Take good care of my lamb," he wrote about his three-year-old son.

Eliza then thought about returning home to Philly. *Uh-oh.* To stave her off, he told Eliza that she shouldn't come because she wasn't feeling well, and that "I am so anxious for a perfect resto-ration of your health that I am willing to make a great sacrifice for it." What a martyr!

He also advised, "Don't alarm yourself nor hurry so as to in-jure either yourself or the children." It's gross stuff. To preempt her from surprising him and Maria in bed, he asked that if she *did* decide to return, "let me know beforehand . . ."

The whole episode is a massive buzzkill. This is Hamilton at his most un-Hamiltonian. How do we square this with the man we know? "It is easy to snicker at such deceit and conclude that Hamilton faked all emotion for his wife, but this would belie the otherwise exemplary nature of their marriage," reasons Cher-now. "His love for her . . . was deep and constant if highly im-perfect. The problem was that no single woman could seem to satisfy all the needs of this complex man with his checkered child-hood." That said, every male adulterer in history could say with a straight face, "I'm a complex man with a checkered childhood."

Why do men get away with this kind of thing? Many years ear-lier, when accused of adultery, Hamilton's mother was *locked in a dungeon*. Yet when a man has an affair it's a "lapse in judgment." A female cheater gets a scarlet "A"; a male cheater gets an eye-roll and a second chance. It's Gender Inequity #3,407.

As smarmy as all of this was, though, so far, it was just your typical affair. Then, a curveball: Maria told him some good news . . . She and her husband were getting back together! Ham-ilton pretended to be happy, fooling no one.

Soon Maria's husband, a sleaze named James Reynolds, sent Hamilton a letter, filled with goofy spelling errors and curious capitalizations:

Instead of being a Friend. you have acted the part of the most Cruelist man in existence. You have made a whole family miserable. now Sir you have bin the Cause of Cooling her affections for me. She was a woman. I should as soon sespect an angiel from heven . . .

The upshot? Blackmail.

By this point Hamilton had guessed their game. "It was easy to understand that he wanted money . . . [and] I resolved to gratify him." Reynolds asked Hamilton for $1,000, which was roughly one third of his annual salary as treasury secretary. He didn't have that kind of cash, but he agreed to pay the scoundrel in two installments.

That should have been the end of it.

Yet this is the problem with blackmail: it never ends. A few weeks later, James Reynolds had the gall to write Hamilton again, saying that his wife wished to see him, and "for my own happiness and hers I have not the Least Objections to your calling, as a friend to Boath of us." *You can screw my wife, but you're going to pay for it.*

Hamilton, amazingly, went along with this. (Historians, baffled, still ponder the reasons. None seem particularly compelling. In some ways it's his great unsolved mystery.) He visited Maria again. And again. And again. Some visits cost $45, some $30. The sessions were documented with letters and receipts. James Reynolds, quite literally, was pimping his wife.

Whenever Hamilton would try to distance himself, Maria would send a letter such as "I shal be miserable till I se you." Hamilton couldn't figure this out—she seemed hot and cold. One minute she pined for him, the next minute she spoke fondly of her husband.

"Her mind at this time was far from being tranquil or consistent," Hamilton lamented, "for almost at the same minute that she would declare her respect for her husband, cry and feel distressed, [the tears] would vanish and levity would succeed, with bitter execrations on her husband."

It was cartoonishly stupid—like a trick Wile E. Coyote would play on the Road Runner. Yet Hamilton kept falling for the ruse. It soon became apparent—even to Hamilton—that Maria was never a damsel in distress, but rather in cahoots with her husband on a long con. He was their mark. The charade lasted for weeks, months, and a *full year* until Hamilton finally had the steel to cut it off, writing Reynolds that it was "utterly out of my power" to pay him, and that "your note is returned." The sorry chapter finally seemed over.

For generations, the Hamilton clan has uneasily grappled with their patriarch's folly. They never found a good explanation. His grandson (Dr. Allan McLane Hamilton, a renowned psychiatrist) thought he found the answer:

To the psychiatrist the matter is simple, for it is a well-known fact that those possessing the highest order of intelligence; professional men, great statesmen . . . manifest at times what can only be looked upon as a species of irresponsibility that accompanies the highest genius, and impulsively plunge into the underworld.

Somewhere Bill Clinton is reading this, nodding his head.

8
LEADERSHIP

SEPARATE THE MERIT FROM THE DRUNKARDS

EMBRACE EQUALITY

—

*"There are strong minds in every walk of life that
will rise superior to the disadvantages of situation
and will command the tribute due to their merit . . .
The door ought to be equally open to all."*

N o Founding Father—not one—is spotless on
the issue of slavery. The debate wasn't as tidy as
North versus South, as even New York City, by
some estimates, had 20 percent of its population
enslaved. No one dared touch the issue. The closet abolitionists
remained in the closet.

That said, the Founders' stances on slavery—and their overall
thoughts on equality, African Americans, and race relations—do
fall on something of a continuum. Toward one end sits Benjamin Franklin, who, in his last public act at age eighty-four,
would spearhead a push for abolition. (Yet even Franklin was
no purist—earlier in life he owned slaves.) Joining him is John
Adams, who called slavery "a foul contagion in the human character." (Yet as Adams's biographer John Ferling notes, "As a lawyer he occasionally defended slaves, but as a politician he made
no effort to loosen the shackles of those in bondage . . . There is

no evidence that he ever spoke out on the issue of slavery in any national forum.")

Thomas Jefferson, it must be said, lands on the other end of the spectrum. And somewhere in between fall Madison, Monroe, and Washington. "There is not a man living who wishes more sincerely than I do to see a plan adopted for the abolition of slavery," Washington said before eventually emancipating his own slaves . . . but only when he died.

And Hamilton? The answer, like always, is complicated. Think back to his upbringing. On the islands of his childhood, "the mortality rate of slaves hacking away at sugarcane under a pitiless tropical sun was simply staggering: three out of five died within five years of arrival," writes Chernow. As a boy, young Alex would see the savagery on the streets—his house sat less than a hundred yards from the slave market. As a young teenager, he would grimly tally up the counts of slaves in the ledger books of his trading shop, participating, in his own passive way, as a slave trader.

One way to look at this is that he always had his hands dirty; another take is that after a courtside seat to barbarism, he found the act repugnant and would therefore advocate, whenever he could, for the rights and emancipation of slaves.

Let's look at his record.

In a shameful clause from the peace treaty that ended the Revolutionary War, the British were banned from "carrying away any Negroes or other property." This spoke to a dark and tragic irony: for many African Americans, the War of Independence had meant freedom at the hands of the "enemy." (When British forces conquered a southern plantation, the slaves were then freed.)

The South couldn't swallow this. Southern leaders demanded that Britain round up and return their slaves, and some owners, unwilling to wait for the paperwork, literally hunted the streets of New York and tried to recapture them.

Hamilton had two reactions.

First: He refused to honor this clause of the peace treaty (that slaves must be returned to their owners), as "[t]hings *odious* or *immoral* are not to be presumed. The abandonment of Negroes . . . to fall again under the yoke of their masters, and into slavery, is as *odious* and *immoral* a thing as can be conceived." This was not a law he could support.

Second: He took action. Along with John Jay, his old college friend Robert Troup, and Aaron Burr, Hamilton formed the New York Society for Promoting the Manumission of Slaves, which gave shelter to freed slaves being chased by their former owners. The group set up a school to educate black students, it waged a PR campaign against slavery, and it petitioned New York to abolish this practice "so repugnant to humanity." The results: mixed. The group did help end slavery in New York, but the law was not passed until 1799, and it was a "gradual" emancipation that did not complete until a full generation later, in 1827.

Hamilton also backed an idea from his old friend, John Laurens, who, during the war, wanted to free southern slaves and let them fight the British. When the plan failed to get through congressional gridlock, Hamilton wrote to Laurens, "There is no virtue [in] America," since the southern states have "fitted their inhabitants for the chain."

Alexander Hamilton is one of the rare Founders who never owned a slave. And while his coarse language makes our modern ears cringe, his message is one of equality: "Their natural faculties are probably as good as ours," he writes. "The contempt we have been taught to entertain for the blacks, makes us fancy many things that are founded neither in reason nor experience."

Let's compare this to some observations from the author of the Declaration of Independence. According to Jefferson:

> [Blacks] are at least as brave, and more adventuresome. But this may perhaps proceed from a want of forethought, which prevents their seeing a danger till it be present. When present, they do not go through it with more coolness or steadiness than the whites.

It gets worse. Ever the philosopher, Jefferson ponders:

> The circumstance of superior beauty, is thought worthy attention in the propagation of our horses, dogs, and other domestic animals; why not in that of man?

Here it comes.

> Besides those of color, figure, and hair, there are other physical distinctions proving a difference of race. They have less hair on the face and body. They secrete less by the kidneys, and more by the glands of the skin, which gives them a very strong and disagreeable odor.

"Lincoln would make Jefferson the grandfather of emancipation, for writing that all men were created equal, and rightly so," notes Brookhiser. "But the racist fantasies that disfigure the *Notes on Virginia*—that black faces show no emotion, that black artists show no talent, that blacks prefer to mate with whites even as orangutans prefer to mate with blacks—looks cracked and shabby next to the plain talk of the colonel from St. Croix."

Still, during the Constitutional Convention, Hamilton never leaped from his chair to demand the end of slavery. Neither did Washington. Neither did Franklin. The issue was toxic. "If there was one explosive device that could blow up the entire national enterprise, this was it, and the delegates knew it," explains Joseph Ellis. "Leadership, as they saw it, meant evading rather than facing the moral implications of the slavery question. Whether this was a failure of moral leadership or a realistic recognition of the politically possible can be debated until the end of time."

FIND THE IMPLIED POWER

—

"There are <u>implied</u> as well as <u>express</u> powers."

W E RETURN TO THE world of banks. (Are you sick of banks yet? Imagine how Thomas Jefferson felt.) And file this one under: *Not sexy, but wildly important.* Opponents of Hamilton's banking bill—led by Jefferson and Madison—argued that the evil banks and the "stock-jobbers" were more than just ugly and British: a federal bank was unconstitutional.

This triggered the nation's first constitutional crisis. Their argument was simple and powerful: if the Constitution doesn't mention a bank, the government can't create a bank.

"The power of erecting banks and corporations was not given to the general government; it remains then with the state itself," Jefferson argued. Then he took it a step further. If anyone acts as an agent of the federal bank, even if they are just working as a "cashier," they will be "adjudged *guilty of high treason and suffer death accordingly.*"

High treason! You have to respect the man's passion. A lot of folks these days hate the bankers on Wall Street, but Thomas Jefferson, quite literally, wanted them killed.

The debate reached a crescendo when the House passed the banking bill, 39 votes to 20, and Washington had just ten days to sign it. He wavered. *Was the bank constitutional?* He considered using the nation's first veto. With the clock ticking, he sent along Jefferson and Madison's arguments to Hamilton, asking for a response.

In a typically Hamiltonian effort, he told Washington he would give it *"a thorough examination"* and then studied, prepped his arguments, wrote, and pulled all-nighters to craft a rebuttal of a staggering 15,000 words—40 dense pages.

Eliza helped him—as she must have done far more often than we know. Decades later, she remembered those hectic nights of research: "He made your government," she later told a young man. "Jefferson thought we ought not to have a bank and President Washington thought so. But my husband said, 'We must have a Bank.' I sat up all night, copied out his writing, and the next morning, he carried it to President Washington and we had a bank."

And all this without Red Bull. The exhausted treasury secretary delivered his treatise the next morning, noting that it had "occupied him the greatest part of last night."

Washington read it carefully. Hamilton argued that the power to create a bank is not *explicit,* but it's clearly *implied* by the Constitution. "It is not denied that there are *implied* as well as *express* powers and that the former are as effectually delegated as the latter," he wrote.

Then, as now, people turned to *The Federalist Papers* as one tool for interpreting the Constitution. The *Papers* state:

> *No axiom is more clearly established in law or in reason
> than that wherever the end is required, the means are au-
> thorized.*

It must have been delicious for Hamilton to note that this particular *Federalist Paper,* number 44, was written by none other
than . . . James Madison.

(By the way, what did Aaron Burr think of all this? When asked
for his take on the one issue that had polarized the nation, Burr
declined to comment, as he had not read the plan "with proper attention." He tended to avoid controversy, which must have driven
Hamilton bonkers. "Is it a recommendation to have *no theory*?"
Hamilton later asked about Burr, exasperated.)

The Constitution, Hamilton argued, clearly gives the government the powers to do things like collect taxes and promote trade.
A bank is a means to those ends, and therefore the power is implied. Washington had seen all he needed to see. He signed the
bill immediately.

Hamilton had done it. Against all odds, he now had his Bank
and the Debt Assumption.

Hamilton gave the government its oomph. His "works and
words have been more consequential than those of any other
American in shaping the Constitution under which we live,"
notes historian Clinton Rossiter.

Scholars and politicians have spent decades and centuries, of
course, debating the pros and cons of a muscular federal government, and the fiery debate will rage as long as there is a United
States. Yet it was Hamilton who lit the match. (And gathered the

kindling and arranged the logs and then wrote a 500-page instruction manual on campfire safety.)

MEANWHILE, AT AARON BURR'S HOUSE . . .

While Hamilton toiled to build America's economy, Aaron Burr, looking for work, decided to run for the Senate. He buttered up the rivals of Hamilton's father-in-law, Senator Philip Schuyler, and ousted the old man. "Burr was the perfect man [to beat Schuyler]," writes Sedgwick. He had "the quality of no quality . . . Burr was no lightning rod, but a broad, flat meadow that didn't offer so much as a single tree to strike." Hamilton fumed. This felt like a betrayal.

Senator Burr kept a low profile. He amused himself by writing a history of the Revolutionary War, flipping through the government archives and sketching out notes. (When Washington heard about this little side project, he banned Burr from the archives.)

Burr would later float his name for vice president in 1792; he received exactly one vote.

So he switched strategies.

In 1795 he rubbed elbows with Thomas Jefferson, suggesting that, with his own neutrality, he could help Jefferson win New York. Jefferson must have been intrigued. So in the election of 1796, Burr came in *fourth* place with 30 electoral votes (Jefferson snagged 68). Somehow, even though he lacked many (or any) signature issues, and as if emerging from thin air, Aaron Burr was on the come-up.

BEING RIGHT TRUMPS BEING POPULAR

—

"I have learned to hold popular opinion of no value."

IMAGINE IF CNN EXISTED in 1790. Every segment would have talking heads saying that "Hamilton has gone too far!" or "Hamilton betrays the troops!" or "90 percent of Americans disapprove of the treasury secretary!"

He would tune this noise out. Like most good leaders, Hamilton refused to be swayed by public opinion, polls, or focus groups.

Let's consider one of his most hated moves as treasury secretary. When America raised its meager army to fight the British, the government couldn't afford to pay the soldiers, so, in many cases, the troops were paid with bonds. IOUs, basically.

The war ended in 1783, but for years the government was broke and couldn't pony up. Those IOUs began to look worthless. Thousands of revolutionary patriots, who had risked their lives to win the nation's freedom, were left clutching scraps of paper that might never be honored. Many sold these IOUs at a dramatically reduced rate—often 20 cents on the dollar. The buyers? Financial speculators—aka the greedy would-be bankers.

Let's break this down, John Oliver style:

Pretend that in 1777, the government pays a soldier with a $100 bond.

1778: The government still can't pay.

1779: Still can't pay.

1780: . . .

1781: . . . (yep, still broke.)

1782: . . . ("Check's in the mail!")

1783: . . .

1784: That same soldier, disgusted, and having lost faith that the no-good government will *ever* make good on the $100 bond, says, *Screw it,* and sells it to whoever will take it.

"I'll give you $20," says a New Yorker wearing a slick suit.

"But . . . it's worth $100," says the soldier.

"Okay. Good luck with that," says the city slicker, turning to leave.

"No! Wait! Fine. I'll take $20." *Better $20 than nothing*, thinks the soldier. They shake hands. Deal.

Now it's 1790. Hamilton turns on the electricity of the nation's financial system, and suddenly, for the first time in a decade, it looks like the bonds will have real value. That $100 bond is now worth something closer to, well, $100.

So who should benefit from this new change of fortune—the patriotic soldiers or the greedy speculators?

You can see where this is headed. Madison ducked the question, saying that he hadn't yet formed "any precise ideas" on the subject. Jefferson, of course, hated the money-men and complained that the speculators were "fraudulent purchasers of this paper."

Public sentiment was clear: the virtuous soldiers had sold those bonds in a moment of desperation, so now we should "do the right thing" and make them whole. Patriots versus Speculators: it seemed clear-cut. (Twitter would side with the soldiers.)

Our man had a different take. He acknowledged that the case "is a hard one," but at the end of the day, the soldiers did, in fact, get cash when they needed it, and the buyers of the bonds did, in fact, assume the risk. Besides, not all the owners of these IOUs were heroic patriots in dire straits; some simply wanted to make a buck. How could you tell the difference?

Hamilton knew it would be a bitter pill, but like always, he went back to the basics. Contracts matter. Not only is the concept right in principle, but it's imperative for establishing the nation's credit. A deal is a deal.

As a young army officer, he had lugged around those economic treatises by Malachy Postlethwayt on the *Universal Dictionary of Trade and Commerce* (remember that?), and he remembered its lessons well: investors need confidence in the markets.

Investors needed to know that if they booked a deal, it wouldn't be later overturned because, well, the public felt sorry for the other guy. Discrimination would be a "breach of faith" that would lead to "a state of bad credit," and the US needed to conquer the credit.

So he ruled decisively *against* the sympathetic soldiers. Done and done.

The audacity of Hamilton's position is almost unimaginable. It would make, say, overhauling Social Security look like child's play. Yet the move established a rock-solid precedent of property rights, something that every American now takes for granted. It reassured investors.

Within a few short years, Hamilton's economy had credit which rivaled that of any nation in Europe. And remember the

Louisiana Purchase? Thomas Jefferson gets credit for the deal of the century, yet it wouldn't have been possible—America couldn't have afforded it—without the foundation laid by Hamilton. Once again he lost the popular vote, and once again he won the vote from history.

COMMAND THE DETAILS

—

"The details of this loan are deficient."

Hamilton commanded every detail of every project. Let's look at two of them: (1) The US Mint; (2) The Coast Guard.

1) THE MINT

For us mortals, an accomplishment like the "founding of the US Mint" would be the triumph of a lifetime. For Hamilton, it barely cracks the top 20.

Yet he knew that without a stable currency—what economists would later call "liquidity"—it's hard to buy or sell goods. Want to buy some eggs for breakfast? You might need to barter a carrot. Or maybe you could pay in British pounds and shillings . . . but every state had a different exchange rate.

The nation needed its own coin. An American dollar.

So Hamilton dug in. He made himself an expert on the science of coins and metals, plunging into each and every detail. When he came up for air, he penned the encyclopedic "Report on the Establishment of a Mint." He laid out the key questions about currency, flashing the classic Hamiltonian logic, including:

- *What ought to be the nature of the money unit of the United States?*
- *What's the proportion and composition of alloy in each kind?*
- *What shall be the number, denomination, sizes, and devices of the coins?*

Should the coins be made of gold, silver, or copper? What weight? What size? How do you peg it to an exchange rate? Hamilton romps through all these questions with a staggering command of the details, sprinkling in data from history, economics, and science. (As a teenager, he had scribbled all those weird facts into his army notebook—it paid off.)

He casually mentions that:

Sir Isaac Newton, in a representation to the treasury of Great Britain, in the year 1717 . . . concludes thus: "By the course of true and exchange between nation and nation, in all Europe, fine gold is to fine silver as $14^4/_5$ or 15 to 1."

He cites economic data from Holland. He drops in some exchange rates in Sweden, Germany, and Denmark. And all this without Google.

Fun fact: the mint introduced a coin even cheaper than the penny—a half-cent piece. Hamilton argued that *the lowest denomination would establish the lowest possible price for goods,* so a half-cent piece would benefit the poor. How many thousands of needy Americans could suddenly, because of this one decision, buy cheaper loaves of bread?

You know how our coins have the busts of US Presidents? Hamilton's idea. He argued this would forge a sense of national identity and serve as "a great safeguard against counterfeits." (Presumably he didn't know his own mug would land on the $10 bill.)

Hamilton's plan was so dazzling, in fact, that it earned some rare praise from his archnemesis. Thomas Jefferson replied, "I return your report on the mint, which I have read over with a great deal of satisfaction."

2) THE COAST GUARD

IN THOSE WOBBLY EARLY DAYS OF the United States, the main source of government revenue—a full 90 percent—was not taxes, but duties on imported goods. (In fact, amazingly, that would be the case until the early twentieth century.) The import duties were a beast to collect. If boaters smuggled in tea without paying the duty, then the fragile US government would remain penniless. How to fix this? "I have under consideration," mused Hamilton, "the business of establishing guard boats."

So he did it. He already had congressional authority to keep "in good repair the lighthouses, beacons, buoys, and public piers in several states." Once again, Hamilton poured himself into the minutiae, suddenly becoming an expert on, of all things, lighthouses. "This towering intellect scrawled more mundane letters about lighthouse construction than any other single subject," notes Chernow, as Hamilton mastered "such excruciating banalities as the best whale oil, wicks, and candles to brighten lighthouse beams."

At Hamilton's urging, Congress passed a bill that would establish a fleet of "revenue cutters," boats that would patrol the waters and, well, guard the coast. (In 1915 they rebranded as the Coast Guard.) Hamilton personally dictated the material of the boats' sails (local cloth), the precise munitions for each vessel (ten muskets, twenty pistols), and required that each boat always have "salted meat with biscuit and water on board" in case of an accident. He left no detail to chance.

Why do some leaders succeed and others fail? There are thousands of books and theories. But one way to be very, very good at your craft is to apply meticulous attention to the details. Take Steve Jobs. He coupled his grand vision with a demanding, almost masochistic streak that obsessed over things like the dimensions of USB ports. This can be annoying. It can also unlock greatness.

In the same way that Jobs fussed over the designs of the stairwells in the Apple stores, Hamilton even micromanaged how the Coast Guard employees should act when they boarded a vessel. "Always keep in mind that their countrymen are free men," he ordered. Coast Guard officers should "therefore refrain . . . from whatever has the semblance of haughtiness, rudeness, or insult." This directive was so on-point, it was still being used in the 1962 Cuban Missile Crisis.

Even to this day, the Coast Guard refers to this as "Hamilton's Charge."

BARKIN' BEATS BITIN'

—

"Whenever the government appears in arms, it ought to appear like a <u>Hercules</u> and inspire respect by the display of strength."

So imagine that you're sitting at the desk of Alexander Hamilton in the early 1790s. You have a Treasury Secretary Checklist:

- ☑ Create the Bank
- ☑ Assume the state's debt
- ☑ Create the US Mint
- ☑ Create the Coast Guard
- ☑ Establish that contracts matter (the IOU thing)
- ☐ Somehow, somewhere, get more revenue.

That last box had yet to be checked. How could the federal government get more revenue? The import duties—now protected by the Coast Guard—were about as high as they could go. Yet without more revenue, the nation would never hope to pay off that staggering debt of $54,124,464.56, plus the $25 million in debt assumed from the states.

This meant only one thing: taxes.

Let's put this in perspective. Today, politicians quibble about whether taxes should go from *x* percent to *y* percent. The debates are about *how much*. Even at the outer fringe of the debate, very few politicians argue that there should be *absolutely no taxes whatsoever.* Yet in the America of 1790, there were no taxes. Hamilton basically proposed the first. Is it any wonder the man was so polarizing?

"Taxes are never welcome to a community," Hamilton admitted, but then gave Congress a bulleted list of items that would need taxes or duties, including:

- *Hats, caps, and bonnets, of every sort.*
- *Gloves and mittens.*
- *Stockings.*
- *Artificial flowers, feathers, and other ornaments for women's headdresses.*
- *Fans.*
- *Dolls, dressed and undressed.*
- *Toys.*
- *Buttons of every kind.*

And the list goes on and on. History has forgotten Hamilton's war on "dolls, dressed and undressed," but there was one item that nearly launched a civil war: spirits. This was the real money-maker. In perhaps the glummest words that Hamilton ever wrote, he argued that "the consumption of ardent spirits is carried to an extreme which is truly to be regretted." (Hamilton liked to pour that second glass. But probably not a seventh.)

It didn't go over well. Congress approved the plan, passing it into law, but much of America wondered, *Wait, didn't we just fight a revolution over taxes?* To those on Team Jefferson, it looked like it was time for another Boston Tea Party.

Whiskey was an especially touchy subject. It came mostly

from Pennsylvania—then thought of as the "western frontier" of the United States—where the rugged Appalachians "claimed that distilling grain into whiskey was the most convenient way of transporting a crop to market," explains Brookhiser. "But the main reason the frontiersmen . . . made whiskey was because they liked to drink it." He reminds us of a moonshiner's song, "Copper Kettle":

My daddy, he made whiskey,
My granddaddy made it too.
We ain't paid no whiskey tax
Since 1792.

As anyone who works for the IRS knows, it's never a hoot to be a tax collector. People don't like you. And the Pennsylvanians really, really didn't like tax collectors. Mobs began to verbally threaten the tax collectors, then strip them naked, tar and feather them, and beat them.

President Washington gave the mob a warning: *Pay the tax. Act orderly.*

The mob took it up a notch. They pulled a knife on one tax collector and threatened to scalp him. The mob *whipped* a tax collector, burned a man's crops, and threatened violence to his wife and children.

Then things took a turn for the worse.

A mob of six thousand whiskey lovers gathered near Pittsburgh, threatening to burn the city to ashes. They built guillotines. They got drunk and rattled their pitchforks and cited the glory of Robespierre, who, in France, had lopped off head after head.

What should the government do? Washington's cabinet was split. The secretary of state wanted to broker a compromise, asking for a "spirit of reconciliation," presumably no pun intended. Hamilton would have none of that. The uprising would need to be quelled. "The very existence of government demands this course," he insisted. "The force ought, if attainable, to be an imposing one."

For Hamilton, this was the ultimate test of whether a nation was truly a nation. If basic laws could not be enforced, he wondered, then what good is the government? Insurrections cannot be tolerated. Mobs cannot rule.

Once again he took up his quill to defend his principles, writing anonymously (this time as "Tully"), "Shall the majority govern or be governed? Shall the nation rule or be ruled? Shall the general will prevail, or the will of a faction?" If the government failed to take decisive action, then a mob was free to stomp on the rights of minorities.

Not on Alexander Hamilton's watch. First he asked politely, then he asked again, but now, he argued, it is time to "exert the full force of the law . . . Moderation enough has been shown; it is time to assume a different tone."

Washington finally agreed. Despite howls of protest, he assembled an army of twelve thousand troops, mostly militiamen from neighboring states. (At the time there was no standing army—something else the Jefferson camp dreaded.)

Washington named it the "Army of the Constitution," winning

the battle of spin. He personally led the force. It remains the only moment in our nation's history when the commander in chief literally headed up the army, not counting Bill Pullman in *Independence Day*.

Hamilton desperately wanted to join the campaign, even though his nominal title, Secretary of the Treasury, had nothing to do with the army. He whipped up a clever argument, suggesting that in government affairs, " 'tis useful that those who propose measures should partake in whatever dangers they may involve." Washington granted the request.

So the two men rode off to battle together, the general and his most trusted aide, just like old times. In vintage form, Hamilton gave precise orders on exactly how the army should be configured, right down to the jackets of the uniforms, which should be of "sufficient length of body to protect well the bowels."

Hamilton didn't want any bloodshed; he wanted a show of force. There's an old expression in the West Indies that perhaps young Alex heard as a child: *Barkin' beats bitin'*. And it worked. Hamilton's army was so large, so "Herculean," that the mob simply melted away. If Hammie had bowed to public pressure and used a more modest force, the mob might have taken their chances and fired their muskets. But an overpowering force of twelve thousand? *No thanks, we'll just pay the tax.*

The Whiskey Rebellion ended in peace. The army took one hundred fifty prisoners and convicted two of treason; they were later pardoned. Crushing the rebellion was the centerpiece of Washington's next State of the Union (ghostwritten, of course, by you-know-who), as it "demonstrated that our prosperity rests on solid foundations."

Once again, Hamilton took the longer view, and once again, his reputation took a pounding. Much of the country seethed. They saw this as one more way for Hamilton—the supposed monarchist—to wrest power for himself. How did Jefferson refer to this episode? "Hamilton's Insurrection."

SEPARATE THE MERIT
FROM THE DRUNKARDS

—

*"A man of real merit is never seen in so favorable a light
as through the medium of adversity; the clouds that
surround him are shades that set off his good qualities."*

I

T'S EASY TO FORGET that, prior to 1776, much of what would
become "America" still functioned like an aristocracy. Especially in the military. If a general had to pick a new captain,
he might choose the idiot who came from a noble family.

This sickened George Washington, who, as a young man, saw
this nepotism when serving in the British army. So his Revolutionary squad was different: he promoted from within, rewarded
merit, and cared less about titles than talent. He passed this along
to Hamilton.

When choosing officers for the treasury department, Hamilton
noted that the candidates were "represented to be men of merit."
In the army, another officer had "a high value for his merits."
Writing to his old friend Lafayette, he remarked that "all those
men are men of merit." He used the word "merit" almost as much
as he did "maxims."

Quick disclaimer: Like most things with the Founding Fathers,
the issue is shaded with nuance. Even Washington made excep-
tions. When Lafayette first volunteered to join the army, for exam-

ple, he had about as much military training as Taylor Swift—but he came with impeccable connections, the lure of French support, and a letter of introduction from Benjamin Franklin. You could argue that in the embryonic USA, merit mattered more than in any culture in history . . . but the privileged still had privileges. Oh, and it goes without saying that "men of merit" are all, well, men. How many thousands and millions of women, with plenty of merit, were underappreciated and overlooked? It was a meritocracy for *some*.

But. Within the smaller universe of white men, Hamilton did seem to value ability over fancy titles. He even shattered tradition by promoting a blue-collar sergeant, an *enlisted* man, to the rank of a commissioned officer. This baffled Congress. "Hamilton's request to promote a sergeant to lieutenant was so unusual," explains Newton, that the New York Convention called upon Hamilton for an explanation. Hamilton fought for the sergeant—and won.

Or take a look at Hamilton's notes from 1798, when he judged a pool of candidates for military promotion. He didn't just delegate this task. He didn't rely on the opinions of others. He jotted the name of each recruit, and then listed his thoughts about their character:

Nathaniel Paulding—Probably a good lieutenant
Timothy—Unworthy
William—Drunkard
Dowe J. Fonda—A good Ensign in the late War, is worthy of
    a Captaincy, but a Majority would be too much now
E— H—Drunkard

B— H—*Drunkard (not certain) but probably of slender
qualifications.*

J— K—*Worthless.*

Benjamin—Unknown

A—R—Gambler

Richard L. Walker—Very violent Jacobin

W— R—*Unworthy*

— *Kirkland—Unknown, probably bad*

—*Drunkard*

The list goes on for a delightful three pages. You can almost
see him inspecting each of the troops, looking them over, asking
them to spin around, examining the shine of their boots and the
cuffs of their uniforms, sniffing for booze on their breath, and
then decreeing, "Drunkard. Worthless." Hamilton was the original Simon Cowell.

THINK SEVEN STEPS AHEAD
—

"[Americans] are essentially businessmen. With us
agriculture is of small account. Commerce is everything."

HAMILTON LOOKED INTO A crystal ball and he saw the future. Specifically, he saw two very clear images: (1) manufacturing; and (2) the military. Let's look at each.

1) THE FUTURE OF MANUFACTURING

IN HAMILTON'S DAY, EIGHT OUT OF every ten Americans were farmers. It seemed like this would never change. Taking a long lens of human history, people worked on the farm for thousands of years; in 200 BC, the average day for a Roman farmer looked an awful lot like the average day for a farmer in 1789. Plant. Hoe. Reap.

Hamilton smelled something different in the air. He had a hunch that America had so much more to offer: innovation, new technologies, and time-wasting games on our smartphones. Still on a hot streak from the national bank, debt assumption, and the Mint, Hamilton lobbed yet another manifesto at Congress: "Report on Manufactures."

Always going back to the core principles, Hamilton made an argument that no one else seemed to have considered: farming takes up only part of the year. The winter months are idle. Thus, manufacturing jobs are "more constant, more uniform, and more ingenious" than the planting of corn.

Besides, the country needed more clothes and more bullets. "The extreme embarrassments of the United States during the late war, from an incapacity of supplying themselves, are still a matter of keen recollection," Hamilton gently reminded his colleagues.

Though it had been "independent" since 1776, America still relied on British imports. Jefferson accused Hamilton of worshipping King George, but the goal of Hamilton's policies, in the end, was to wean the baby nation *off* Britain's teat. The War of Independence, in his mind, was not yet over: the nation needed *economic* independence.

Hamilton launched the Society for Establishing Useful Manufactures, or SUM. Now channeling his inner Tony Stark, he created a futuristic town that would serve as a laboratory, of sorts, for the growth of American industry. Think of it as the great-grandfather to Google Labs. They found a spot in Great Falls, New Jersey, that would become the city of Paterson. The town would have "cotton mills, a textile printing plant, a spinning and weaving operation, and housing for fifty workers."

Why all the fuss? Hamilton argued that, unlike farming, manufacturing offers:

- *"Additional employment to classes of the community not ordinarily engaged in the business."* Yep, this (finally) includes women.

- *"The promoting of emigration from foreign countries."*
  Specifically, European immigrants would be eager to "pur-
  sue their own trades and professions." This is precisely what
  happened.
- *"The furnishing greater scope for the diversity of talents
  and dispositions which discriminate men from each other."*
  His point here: *Hey, not everyone wants to grow potatoes.
  Why not let people choose the jobs that fit their talents?*
  This will allow the welders to be welders, the farmers to be
  farmers, and the poets to be Starbucks baristas.

SUM had a rocky start, nearly killed by the financial panics in
1791 and 1792. Then something funny happened. Paterson trans-
formed into a hotbed of innovation for the next century—it built
locomotive factories, the first submarines, hydroelectric plants,
the first Colt guns, and the engine for Charles Lindbergh's *Spirit
of St. Louis*.

2) THE FUTURE OF THE MILITARY

THE FIRST QUESTION REALLY SHOULD BE "What military?" The nation had none. At the close of the Revolutionary War, the army
had been all but disbanded, reduced to a tiny force (eight hundred) that could fit inside a single Kmart. What if England attacked again? France? Spain? So many things could go wrong.

Yet no one else seemed troubled by this, as "standing armies"
were the great bugaboo of Republicans. Jefferson felt that standing armies meant Caesar, and Caesar meant tyranny. "There shall
be no standing army but in time of actual war," said Jefferson,
as they are "inconsistent with [a people's] freedom." Jefferson

wanted to abolish the army in the Bill of Rights. As for James Madison? His plan for military vigor, at one point, was to rent a navy from Portugal.

To Hamilton this seemed like madness. He had spilled too much blood in the Revolutionary War and he had seen his friends killed. (RIP, John Laurens.) America would again be dragged into a war, and "a nation, despicable by its weakness, forfeits even the privilege of being neutral." This seems perfectly reasonable to our modern eyes—no one on the Left or the Right, Democrat or Republican, is calling for the dissolution of the US Army—but in 1798 it had, for the Jeffersonian crew, the whiff of tyranny.

Even many Federalists hated the army. Befuddled, John Adams considered Hamilton's idea for an army "one of the wildest extravagances of a knight errant," and "proved to me that Mr. Hamilton knew no more of the sentiments and feelings of the people of America than he did those of the inhabitants of one of the planets." Fair. Hamilton really *was* out of step with popular opinion, but when has that ever stopped him?

Yet the overall mindset is useful in any job, any industry, any phase in life. Let the chumps think about Tuesday: you think about next year or even next decade. Wayne Gretzky, whether he knew it or not, lived by Hamilton's maxim. When someone asked the greatest hockey player of all time what made him so good, he said, "Skate to where the puck is going, not where it has been."

PRESIDENT HAMILTON?

Alexander Hamilton was not technically born in the United States, of course, so was he even eligible to be President?

There's a little-known loophole.

The fine print of the Constitution states that the President must be native born "or a Citizen of the United States, at the time of the Adoption of this Constitution." By 1787, Hamilton was a US citizen. He was in.

President Hamilton. That has a nice ring to it. Just imagine the State of the Union addresses that would last for six hours, filled with references to the Dutch economy, the recipe for crystal glass, and the calculations of Isaac Newton.

But maybe he never actually *wanted* the job. After poring through thousands of pages of letters and primary sources, Rand Scholet concludes, "Hamilton never expressed an interest in the Presidency, even to his closest friends." And even if he did, the timing was never right:

1788: Washington's first term.

1792: Washington's second term.

1796: Even Hamilton acknowledged that John Adams was the "heir apparent."

1800: This, theoretically, could have been Hamilton's rightful turn. Yet by then, half the country hated his bank.

But he was only forty-four years old! The wind could change once again. Maybe if Hamilton bided his time, lay low, and re-habilitated his image, he could later mount a comeback. Yet as we know by now, Hamilton was not a man who could lie low . . .

PRESERVE ORDER
THROUGH PUNISHMENT

—

"Have one half of his head shaved, and one eye-
brow; and be publicly drummed out of the
garrison with a halter round his neck."

A GOOD LEADER SHOULD INSPIRE. That's an upbeat message that translates cleanly to business books, career guides, and Broadway blockbusters. Yet a great leader, at times, must also do something that rarely gets a chorus: mete out punishment.

Hamilton knew that if you allowed things to slide, then people would soon take advantage. He did what was necessary to preserve order. In the Revolutionary War, if his troops deserted, he had them court-martialed or shot. (This was standard protocol for the army. Stern but fair.)

Later, as Inspector General of the army, Hamilton once learned that a private was guilty of desertion. How should the man be punished? Hamilton gave the matter some serious thought. Then he spelled out the exact punishment with astonishing specificity:

He [should] receive ninety-nine lashes upon his naked back, at three different times, within two days, thirty-three lashes at each time.

That's a lot of lashing! But maybe it's not enough? Maybe he needs something more . . . memorable? Perhaps he could make the man look like a *Batman* villain?

> *Have one half of his head shaved, and one eye-brow; and be publicly drummed out of the garrison with a halter round his neck, and rendered incapable ever again to serve in the army of the United States.*

Half his head shaved! With a "halter round his neck"!

Hamilton, though, was not confident that this was the optimal means of punishment, and notes:

> *Whether whipping and a discharge from the service, even in the most disgraceful manner, is the mode of punishment best calculated to prevent the crime of desertion, is a question which demands the consideration of future Courts Martial.*

Hamilton wasn't a sadist who enjoyed this kind of stuff. (Yet we have to give him points for creativity.) He disgraced the soldier for a reason: if he is publicly shamed, then other soldiers would be less likely to desert. That would save lives.

Some of the lessons in this book are more subtle, implied, and shouldn't be taken literally. Some of them, however, can be explicitly applied to your daily life—this is obviously the latter. Next time you need to punish an employee who missed a deadline, shave half his head and exactly one eyebrow.

LEARN FROM YOUR ENEMIES

—

"The British system is 'the most perfect government which ever existed.'"

THE WHISKEY TAX. THE banking system. A standing army. All of these concepts, in fairness, did not originate from the mind of Alexander Hamilton—he stole them from Great Britain and the rest of Europe. This is to his credit. He made no apologies for borrowing the concepts that had worked in the Old World.

The other Founders blanched at anything that had a British odor, but Hamilton said if it works, it works.

Jefferson found this appalling, and the enmity ran deep. At a dinner party with Jefferson, Hamilton supposedly described the British system as "the most perfect government which ever existed." At another dinner, according to a book of gossip that Jefferson put together decades later—the wonderfully titled *Anas*—Hamilton (allegedly) said that "there was no stability, no security in any kind of government but a monarchy."

Why does all this matter? It's crucial for understanding how, and why, Hamilton was so unpopular. He was a realist. If the British happened to have a better banking system, why not raid their playbook? "Unlike Jefferson, Hamilton never saw the creation of America as a magical leap across a chasm to an entirely new landscape, and he always thought the New World had much to learn from the Old," summarizes Chernow.

Nations can learn from other nations, firms can learn from their competitors, artists can be inspired by their rivals, and even athletes can steal from their opponents. In the mid-2000s, after watching constant footage of Dirk Nowitzki, Kobe Bryant added the step-back "kick" jump shot to his arsenal. That doesn't make him a Mavericks fan.

HIDE NOTHING

—

"It is certain that I have made every exertion in my power, at the hazard of my health, to comply with the requisitions of the House as early as possible."

I F YOU HAD TO do an ESPN-style Power Rankings of the Founding Fathers in the 1790s, there's little debate that George Washington would come in #1, and Alexander Hamilton #2. He had more juice than Jefferson. More clout than Adams, Madison, or Monroe. We forget this because he was never elected President, but in the fiery crucible of America's inception, there was no one more influential than Alexander Hamilton.

Yet to Hamilton's enemies, it seemed like "His Holiness," as some called him, was running the country. Banks, debt, currency, the Coast Guard, taxes, military force, a strong Executive—what Hamilton wanted, Hamilton got. One Jefferson-backed newspaper charged that Hamilton "fancies himself the great pivot upon which the whole machine of government turns."

So Congress decided enough was enough. *Surely the banks are corrupt, the system is corrupt, Hamilton is corrupt.* After all, only Hamilton seemed to understand all the financial wizardry.

Who was checking up on *him*? Surely his hand must be in the cookie jar?

In December of 1792, as Hamilton no doubt wanted to spend Christmas with Eliza and Philip and the kids, Congress demanded that he provide a detailed reconciliation of all his bookkeeping. So he worked through the holidays and opened his books, showing them all the documentation.

They found nothing wrong.

Not good enough, Congress said. They demanded more details. "By design, these [inquiries] made massive, nay overwhelming, demands on Hamilton," explains Chernow. "He had to furnish a complete reckoning of balances between the government and the central bank, as well as a comprehensive list of sinking-fund purchases of government debt." (Meanwhile, these demands were all secretly orchestrated by Thomas Jefferson, who saw his own influence wane.) "Taking advantage of a short, four-month congressional session, the House gave Hamilton an impossible March 3 deadline." It was an ambush.

Apparently they had never met Alexander Hamilton.

Knowing he was under siege, and sensing that the entire fate of his financial system was at stake, the treasury secretary worked day and night, as always, to prepare his report. Hamilton's critics had "seriously underrated his superhuman stamina." He did not file his report on March 3, the impossible deadline they requested.

He filed two weeks early.

The 21,000-word report came with a suite of detailed, anal-retentive tables and the eighteenth-century version of spreadsheets. He hid nothing. "It is certain that I have made every exertion in my power, at the hazard of my health, to comply with the requisitions of the House as early as possible," he wrote, somehow biting back sarcasm.

Congress hunted for wrongdoing, sifted through all the numbers, poked at every table . . . and found nothing. There was not a lick of evidence that Hamilton had moved a nickel or penny (or half penny) out of place. Yet *still* they remained suspicious.

So Hamilton, of his own volition, suggested that they open yet another inquiry. Again he opened his books. Again they found nothing.

Team Jefferson now realized that they couldn't beat Hamilton, it seemed, by playing it by the book. They would try and find another way.

Things were about to get nasty.

9
OFFICE POLITICS

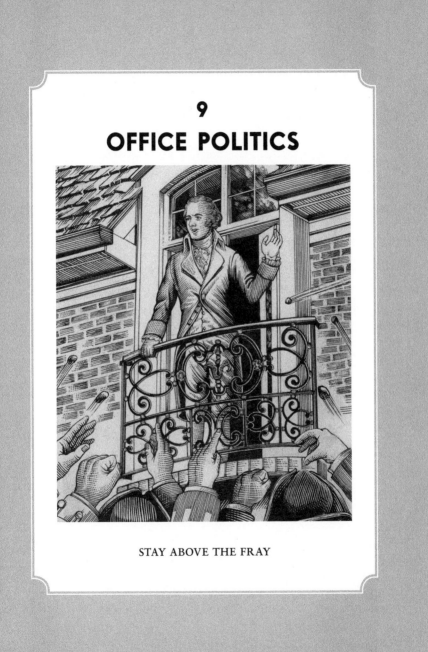

STAY ABOVE THE FRAY

PUBLISH OR PERISH

—

"Fact."

Poor Thomas Jefferson. He couldn't catch a break. He lost the banks, lost the debt, and lost nearly every battle with Hamilton. He would need to get craftier. He grabbed his loyal sidekick, James Madison, and went on a leisurely boating trip through upstate New York, ostensibly to hunt squirrels, go fishing, study insects, and collect natural specimens.

Yet they had a sneaky agenda: to woo the upstate New Yorkers who might share their anti-bank sentiments, including, most likely, Aaron Burr. While on this fishing trip, they had breakfast with a young poet named Philip Freneau, and they gave the poet an offer: Would he care to start a newspaper that could attack Hamilton?

Perhaps Freneau hesitated, or perhaps he said he needed more money, because Jefferson sweetened the deal by offering a cushy job in the State Department as his "translator," even though Freneau spoke only one language, French, which Jefferson spoke as well. The secretary of state assured the poet that this boondoggle job "gives so little to do as not to interfere with any other calling the person may choose." Slick.

This type of trickery infuriated Hamilton, who, ever eager to defend his honor, preferred to shout his opinions from the rooftops. Jefferson was more cunning. He operated behind the scenes, letting others do the dirty work, speaking about as often as Luke Skywalker in *The Force Awakens*.

Freneau happily accepted this "job" and launched the *National Gazette*, a paper that made no pretense of objectivity. Referring to Jefferson as "the colossus of liberty," the paper's sole reason for existence was to take down Hamilton.

And thus began "The Newspaper War." The paper critiqued him, mocked him, and even aped him with poetry:

Public debts are public curses
In soldiers' hands! Then nothing worse is!
In speculators' hands increasing
Public debt's a public blessing!

(That must have *owned* back in the day.)

The *Gazette* blasted Hamilton and his programs, calling them "hereditary monarchy in another shape." Then Freneau took it up a notch, publishing an *Onion*-esque "Rules for changing a limited republican government into an unlimited [monarchy]," and then listed, as its Rules for Monarchy, the tenets of Hamilton's banking system.

Hamilton, in other words, was getting clobbered on social media. So he opened up his eighteenth-century version of Twitter and fired back.

He called out Freneau, pointing out that his job as "translator" was a crock. He called out Jefferson, accusing him of betraying

Washington while serving in the administration. "Is it possible that Mr. Jefferson, the head of a principal department of the government, can be the patron of a paper, the evident object of which is to decry the government and its measures?" Hamilton signed this essay "An American."

(On a sunnier note, the pseudonym does give a glimpse into Hamilton's evolution as an immigrant. As a collegian, he had penned his famous essays defending the Boston Tea Party as "A Friend to America." Now he was "An American.")

Things got ugly. One newspaper called Hamilton "a cowardly assassin, who strikes in the dark, and securely wounds, because he is unseen." Hamilton soon had the boldness to suggest that Washington boot Jefferson from office.

Washington, grinding his teeth and exasperated by his two most gifted lieutenants, asked both secretaries to stop the bickering. Hamilton refused to keep quiet. He wrote more anonymous essays, sometimes as "Anti-Defamer," sometimes as "A Plain Honest Man." Like someone ranting on Twitter at 2 a.m., he just couldn't help himself.

At times he even *wrote* a bit like future Internet commenters. Consider an essay he wrote called "Fact No. 1." He mocked Jefferson's inconsistencies on taxation—"a certain description of men are for getting out of debt, yet are against all taxes for raising money to pay it off"—and then, incredibly, he closed the essay with a one-word paragraph:

Fact.

He actually wrote that! As anyone who has spent too much time on Reddit knows, commenters love to state an opinion and then say, "Fact."

The tactics worked. "Hamilton's anonymous newspaper campaign against Jefferson at the height of their opposition was thus infuriatingly difficult to counter," explains Joanne Freeman. "Without the investment of his name, Hamilton could not be held responsible, yet everyone knew him to be the author, giving his essays the authority of his name. It was a win-win situation for Hamilton; either he would compel Jefferson or his defenders to oppose the government in print, or he would reign victorious through Jefferson's silence."

Jefferson called in reinforcements. "Hamilton is really a colossus to the anti-republican party," he was forced to admit. "Without numbers, he is a host within himself." He begged Madison to confront Hamilton. "For god's sake, my dear Sir, take up your pen, select the most striking heresies, and *cut him to pieces* in the face of the public."

Once again operating behind the scenes, the author of the Declaration of Independence orchestrated six essays called "Vindication of Mr. Jefferson"—five were written by James Monroe, one by James Madison.

So for those scoring at home, Hamilton now battled the combined firepower of:

The 3rd President (Jefferson)
The 4th President (Madison)
The 5th President (Monroe)

Oh, and around this time, he clashed sabers with John Adams, the 2nd President.

But the future Presidents had failed. They hadn't managed to topple Hamilton's systems or muzzle his influence.

Hamilton: 1

Future Presidents of the United States: 0

Fact.

STAY ABOVE THE FRAY

—

"[I will] fight the whole 'detestable faction,' one by one."

IN 1795, WHEN HAMILTON cracked opened the nation's financial books and did his math, he must have smiled. His plan had worked. He had done his job well.

The nation's credit? The best in the world. The economy? Humming. "As if by magic," explains Richard Sylla, "by 1795 the United States had in place all the key elements of a modern financial system: stable public finances and national debt management, a dollar currency convertible into hard money, a banking system, a central bank, securities markets, and a host of corporations. In 1789, it lacked every one of them."

So at age thirty-eight, Hamilton resigned his post as treasury secretary on his own terms. (It makes for good drama on Broadway, but he was not, in fact, fired by John Adams.) He quit for a very simple reason: he needed to make real money again. In something of a humblebrag, he observed that "our [nation's] finances are in a most flourishing condition. Having contributed to place those of the nation on a good footing, I go to take a little care of my own."

He went back to his law office, working long hours to support Eliza and Philip and the kids. This astonished many onlook-ers. Late one night, Talleyrand, the French diplomat, walked by Hamilton's law office and was stunned to see him working by candlelight. He was baffled that "a man who made the fortune of his country" was now "working all night in order to support his family."

Yet Hamilton could never escape politics. When tensions flared with Britain, Washington asked him for advice. Hamilton outlined the strategy that would become the Jay Treaty, and then urged Washington to sign it. John Jay's treaty made plenty of em-barrassing concessions to King George, but for Hamilton, one fact trumped everything else: the treaty meant peace.

It also bought the young—and still-developing—nation time. "With peace, the force of circumstances will enable us to make our way sufficiently fast in trade," Hamilton argued. "War at this time would give a serious wound to our growth and prosperity."

The public saw things differently. *Didn't we just fight a war against the British?* The public even turned on George Wash-ington. As John Adams recalled, the President's house was "sur-rounded by an innumerable multitude from day to day, buzzing, demanding war against England, cursing Washington."

(Perspective: Even *George Washington* had a spell with low approval ratings. We bemoan the current state of American poli-tics, lament the nation's divisiveness, but as a philosopher once said, "The good ol' days weren't always good, and tomorrow's not as bad as it seems.")

Someone even graffitied a wall, saying, "Damn John Jay. Damn everyone that won't damn John Jay. Damn everyone that won't put up lights in the windows and sit up all night damning John Jay."

What could Hamilton do?

He would address the public. In person. He arranged for a public discussion of the Jay Treaty on the steps of City Hall. A frisky crowd gathered—five thousand people, jostling shoulder to shoulder, somehow squeezed into the crowded streets. The crowd heckled. The crowd shouted.

Hamilton climbed onto a stoop so the crowd could see him, raised his voice, and then gave a speech that argued for "the necessity of a *full discussion* before the citizens could form their opinions." As one newspaper reported, the crowd could barely hear him on account of the "hissings, coughing, and hootings."

You can imagine Hamilton's disappointment. *This is democracy? This is what I've been fighting for?* He kept speaking, kept trying to appeal to reason, kept trying to instill order. Perhaps he thought back to the time when, as a young revolutionary in college, he had faced down the mob and saved the life of Myles Cooper.

Not this time. The crowd did more than jeer—they started throwing "a volley of stones." On the streets of New York—the very streets where he had fought the British in the Revolutionary War, the very streets that he had turned into a financial mecca—citizens now *threw rocks* at Alexander Hamilton. Somehow he kept his sense of humor, allegedly telling the crowd, "If you use such knock-down arguments, I must retire."

As one Federalist later quipped, the crowd tried to "knock out Hamilton's brains to reduce him to an equality with themselves."

Jefferson later caught wind of this democracy in action, giddily telling Madison that the crowd "appealed to stones and clubs and beat him and his party off the ground."

So did Hamilton go home and cut his losses?

Flashing the same devil-be-damned attitude that he showed while jabbing his bayonet on the fields of Yorktown, he charged *into the streets* and made himself even more of a target. He called out specific critics. He tried to stop a shouting match. He suggested that people move their debate indoors, where they could calmly discuss the issues. He was mocked as an "abettor of Tories"—a charge that goes back to his young lawyering days—so Hamilton challenged the man to a duel.

He wasn't finished.

With blood likely dripping down his forehead, he continued to argue with the rabble-rousers. One witness remembered that "Hamilton then stepped forward, declaring that . . . he would fight the whole party one by one." The witness, astonished, even repeats it for emphasis. "He threw up his arm and declared that he was ready to *fight the whole 'detestable faction' one by one.'*" Hamilton allegedly used "language that would have become a street bully." This led to a *second duel* challenge within the hour.

So Hamilton had agreed to two duels within a single hour. These duels were later settled over correspondence, in a careful negotiation, without pistols and without bloodshed. This is how it usually worked. But as Hamilton would soon learn, not always . . .

HAMILTON: REPUBLICAN OR DEMOCRAT?

Both. Neither. It's nearly impossible to classify the political parties of the 1790s by the terms of today's politics. There's no easy fit. For starters, the "Republicans" of the 1790s were technically called "Democratic Republicans," further scrambling the picture.

It's tricky and dangerous to try to assign Hamilton's policies to a Republican or Democrat, but it's safe to say that, at the very least, both the Left and the Right can claim some views as their own. On the Republican side, Hamilton wanted a strong military, economic growth, and a business-friendly government. On the Democratic side, Hamilton wanted a strong central government, regulations, and funding to spur industry and innovation. "Modern conservatives would distrust his trust in government; modern liberals would find him lacking in compassion," notes Brookhiser.

Then again, both the Left and the Right seem to be coming around. On the progressive end, Paul Krugman praises Hamilton's "pathbreaking economic policy manifestos," which remain "amazingly relevant today." On the conservative side? "There's an elegant memorial in Washington to Jefferson, but none to Hamilton," notes George Will. "However, if you seek Hamilton's monument, look around. You are living in it. We honor Jefferson, but live in Hamilton's country."

LET OTHERS TAKE THE CREDIT
—

*"That man does not know he has asked
me to purchase my own work."*

BACK IN 1792, AT the end of Washington's first term, our first President had mulled over the idea of an early retirement. Who can blame him? So he asked Madison to whip up a Farewell Address, which Madison did, and then it sat in his desk for another four years.

Now, in 1796, Washington was serious—*I'm out.* He kicked the original draft to Hamilton (now a lawyer again), instructing his old protégé to either:

1) Update and tweak Madison's draft; or
2) Start from scratch and "throw the *whole* into a different form."

So of course Hamilton did both. He created one version that simply updated and revised Madison's, and one version that gutted the doc and started from scratch. He showed both versions to the President. Washington preferred Hamilton's "greatly." The only problem, Hamilton being Hamilton, was its length: Washington observed that it wouldn't fit in "all the columns of a large gazette."

They worked together to trim it, tweak it, perfect it. In some ways it sprinkled in his life's great theme: "Cultivate, also, industry and frugality." *Cultivate industry.* That's about as Hamiltonian as it gets.

The Farewell Address was never actually spoken by Washington; it appeared only in written form. The document first appeared, oddly, in a Philadelphia newspaper called *Claypoole's American Daily Advertiser.* (You're not a subscriber?) Others reprinted it.

While the Jefferson-led Republicans thought it was too anti-French—one paper called it "the loathings of a sick mind"—the address, of course, would go down as an iconic American document. Congress read it every year on Washington's birthday, and it helped guide America's foreign policy for decades.

Hamilton never asked for credit.

That wasn't his style. For most of his career he toiled behind the scenes, without fanfare, letting others snatch the glory. For years people speculated as to the Farewell Address's true authorship, but decades later, Eliza revealed, "The whole of the 'Address' was read to me by him as he wrote it and a greater part, if not all, was written by him in my presence." Yet Hamilton kept quiet.

Think back to the Battle of Monmouth, where Hamilton was in a "frenzy of valor" and had cried out, "I will stay with you, my dear General, and die with you!" He didn't gloat. When Hamilton wrote about the battle he barely mentions his own involvement, simply stating that his horse had been shot by a musket ball.

"That is all he wrote about himself," notes Newton. "He wrote nothing about his days reconnoitering prior to the battle nor did he mention his many actions during the conflict itself." Or take the climactic battle of the war: Yorktown. Despite his own heroics—he charged with a bayonet, with no bullets!—he petitioned Congress to award medals for his troops, not for himself.

This is one more reason that, for over two centuries, we never heard much about Hamilton—he didn't like to brag. "There is not a letter or published paper of his that indicates the existence of the least vanity or boastfulness," argues Hamilton's grandson. (A biased source, but still.) "In fact, he never indulged in self-exploitation, but as a rule submerged himself."

Hamilton preferred to let the work speak for itself, which is useful advice for anyone. It's better to get the job right than to get the credit. He knew the truth, and that was enough. On the streets of downtown Manhattan, a man once tried to sell him a copy of the Farewell Address—it was literally sold in the streets—and a bemused Hamilton turned to Eliza and said, "That man does not know he has asked me to purchase my own work."

JUMP AHEAD OF THE SCANDAL

—

"My real crime is an amorous connection with his wife . . ."

REMEMBER JAMES REYNOLDS? A blackmailer never truly goes away, just like a bad penny, the Rolling Stones, and herpes. Maria Reynolds's husband was crooked, and he soon found himself tossed in jail for an unrelated matter (swindling $400 out of a Revolutionary War soldier). If Reynolds had accepted his prison sentence and quietly served his time, then Alexander Hamilton's life might have turned out very differently.

James Reynolds had a different plan. Knowing that he had a get-out-of-jail-free card, the grifter hinted that he "had it in his power to hang the Secretary of the Treasury." He wasn't wrong. The blackmailer, of course, had the paper receipts from Hamilton's sexual trysts—$45 here, $30 there. Because Reynolds was *also* involved in a separate embezzling scandal—involving one of Hamilton's friends, William Duer—to any reasonable observer, this looked like proof of financial fraud.

The details get weedy pretty quick, but essentially, Reynolds was freed from jail and the receipts made their way into the hands of three enemies of Hamilton: Abraham Venable, Frederick

Muhlenberg, and James Monroe. The three men read the receipts and mulled over the damning evidence, before concluding *Hamilton's a crook*.

They thought about bringing the matter immediately to George Washington, but first they agreed, as a courtesy, to confront Hamilton in person. (In the musical, Miranda wisely condenses the story so that Jefferson, Madison, and Aaron Burr confront Hamilton. That's the smart dramatic move, but it never happened.)

James Monroe and friends showed Hamilton the documents. *Ah ha! What do you say to this, good sir?*

Guilty, said Hamilton. *But not of what you think.* He soon confessed that the damning letters had, in fact, come from his quill, but they were evidence of sexual blackmail, not financial misconduct.

He spoke at length (it *is* Hamilton) about the sexual tryst, almost as if confessing his sins. It was an awkward meeting. You can imagine James Monroe glancing at his pocket watch, shifting uncomfortably, as Hamilton shared the story of his troubled sex life. At one point they told him *Please stop talking.* Yet Hamilton kept going. He later recalled, "I insisted upon going through the whole and did so."

Finally the meeting was over. The three enemies, grudgingly satisfied (for now) that there was no financial misconduct, agreed to let the matter drop. "Our suspicions were removed," Monroe remembered. They left Hamilton's place and probably took cold showers. The original documents were kept by Monroe, who promised to keep them a secret.

The secret lasted for no more than twenty-eight hours, when Jefferson learned of the affair, and the letters were eventually leaked to a tabloid monger named James Thomson Callender, who, at the time, functioned as a Jefferson lackey. (Years later, Jefferson referred to him as "a poor creature . . . drunken, penniless, and unprincipled." In other words, a member of the mainstream media.)

At last, thought Jefferson. He had found the chink in Hamilton's armor. Callender (backed by Jefferson) hinted that he would soon expose the Reynolds letters in the press, and that the public would see "this master of morality [confess] that he had an illicit correspondence with another man's wife."

Hamilton felt the noose tightening. One friend warned him that "the throat of your political reputation is to be cut, *in Whispers.*"

Even worse, Callender whispered that Hamilton's true crime wasn't just a sexual affair, but something far more serious: financial mismanagement. All those receipts *must* have referred to financial matters, right? Surely there was more to it than sex, as "so much correspondence could not refer exclusively to wenching."

Keep in mind the larger context. In modern times, bonking another man's wife—while you are married—seems a tad worse than "financial misconduct." But put yourself in Hamilton's shoes. For years he had struggled to tame America's finances. He *was* the bank. Congress still threatened to overturn his system and "uproot it, tree and branch." So if he went down on financial misconduct, perhaps the entire system would buckle? It might have. "It is a maxim," he once wrote, "that no character, however upright, is a match for constantly reiterated attacks, however false." So he would confront the whisperers; he would jump ahead of the scandal. Better to be guilty of Bad Bonking than Bad Banking.

He followed his old and trusty maxim: Speak the truth. *All* of the truth. Say what you believe, no matter the cost. It worked before, right? He had written daring manifestos to defend the Boston Tea Party, to defend the Constitution, to defend his banking system. He risked his life to speak up for Myles Cooper against the mob. It would work. It always worked. So he wrote a ninety-five-page manifesto that exposed the entire affair.

Always fond of snappy titles, he called the treatise "Observations on Certain Documents Contained in No. V & VI of 'The History of the United States for the Year 1796,' in Which the Charge of Speculation Against Alexander Hamilton, Late Secretary of the Treasury, Is Fully Refuted. Written by Himself."

Deep breath. "The charge against me is a connection with one James Reynolds for purposes of improper pecuniary speculation," he began. "My real crime is an amorous connection with his wife."

And here it comes.

In front of the entire young nation, on August 31, 1797, Hamilton published all the juicy details: how Maria had come to his door, invited him upstairs, and later slept in his and Eliza's bed. In full Hamiltonian disclosure, he revealed everything except the number of times that each of them orgasmed. It's almost like he was doing a one-on-one with Barbara Walters, hoping that a full confession would silence his critics and put the matter to bed. "Even now," marvels Brookhiser, "in an era of gossip as reporting and confession as spectator sport, the Reynolds pamphlet remains the frankest admission of adultery by any major American politician."

He kept going. "I can never cease to condemn myself for the pang which it may inflict in a bosom eminently entitled to all my gratitude, fidelity, and love," he wrote, acknowledging his betrayal to Eliza. "But that bosom will approve that even at so great an expense, I should effectually wipe away a more serious stain." *Trust me, my wife will understand.*

In the cruelest twist, even Eliza was openly mocked. The *Aurora* newspaper (backed by Jefferson) wrote, "Art thou a wife?" . . . See him, whom thou has chosen for the partner of this life, lolling in the lap of a harlot!" (Is there anything dumber than these "blame the wife" tropes?)

To some, it seemed that the pamphlet only made the scandal worse. Not only did it embarrass himself and wound Eliza, it made the financial charges look even *more* likely. One tabloid mocked Hamilton by paraphrasing, "I have been [grossly charged with] being a speculator, whereas I am only an adulterer. I have not broken the eighth commandment . . . it is only the seventh which I have violated." Callender sneered, "[The] whole proof in this pamphlet rests upon an illusion. 'I am a rake and for that reason I cannot be a swindler.'"

Hamilton's biggest fan, Angelica, came to his aid with a partial defense. "Merit, virtue, and talents must have enemies and [are] always exposed to envy so that, my dear Eliza, you see the penalties attending the position of so amiable a man," she wrote her sister, choosing to focus her wrath on Hamilton's critics. "All this you would not have suffered if you had married into a family less *near the sun*. But then [you would have missed] the pride, the pleasure, the nameless satisfactions." It's almost the logic of an NBA wife—yes, you have to deal with the cheating, but you get your own Gulfstream jet.

So what can we learn from all this?

From a PR perspective, while it is, in theory, a smart idea to preemptively manage a scandal, the move is not a panacea. Sometimes *I'm sorry* just won't cut it. Hamilton made the same mistake that's made by millions of adulterers: thinking that "telling the truth" will magically make things better.

Then again . . . we'll never know the answer to this, but theoretically, it's possible that the pamphlet *did* work exactly as intended. Hamilton must have known that he would be ridiculed. Yet he feared an even greater catastrophe: that Congress would exploit the receipts and pillage his financial system. This gave him a Pyrrhic victory. His reputation took a hit, but his bank—and our economy—survived.

Another takeaway: Some cheaters think that if they confess an affair, that earns points for "doing the right thing" and will help absolve them of their guilt. It's not that simple. The "truth" can have grim consequences to more people than yourself. Even if Hamilton succeeded in defending his good name—this is debatable—it must have wounded his family.

Amid all the heartache, the Hamiltons received a welcome boost from an old friend: George Washington. The old mentor sent Hamilton a wine cooler (right?!) with a note that was timed to lift the family's spirits:

As a token of my sincere regard and friendship for you, and as a remembrance of me, I pray you to accept a wine cooler . . . [I] present my best wishes, in which Mrs. Washington joins me, to Mrs. Hamilton and the family . . . with every sentiment of the highest regard, I remain your sincere friend, and affectionate Humble Servant.

LET NO GOOD CRISIS GO TO WASTE

—

"If well managed, this affair will turn to good account."

I F YOU GIVE ALEXANDER HAMILTON a lemon, he'll give you lemonade . . . and then a 50,000-word treatise on how lemonade stands can galvanize the economy. Every crisis, for Hamilton, becomes an opportunity. Think back to the beginning. As a teenager in the West Indies, he used a hurricane to catapult himself to New York. As a young man, he used the Revolutionary War to rise above his station. As treasury secretary, he used the Whiskey Rebellion to flex the muscle of federal power.

And in May of 1798, a new crisis emerged: a looming war with France. The French had attacked the boats of US merchants, which Hamilton saw as "too much humiliation." It was time to draw a red line.

Hamilton, now technically a private citizen, suggested that Congress raise an army. They approved ten thousand troops, which galled an incredulous President John Adams, who seethed that "such was the influence of Mr. Hamilton in Congress that, without any recommendation from the President, they passed a bill to raise an army." Even in the wake of the Reynolds affair, Hamilton still had juice.

So who would lead this army? Timothy Pickering (the new secretary of state) described three different chats he had with President Adams.

ADAMS: Whom shall we appoint commander in chief?
PICKERING: Colonel Hamilton.

[A day later]

ADAMS: "Whom shall we appoint commander in chief?"
PICKERING: Colonel Hamilton.

[A day later]

ADAMS: "Whom shall we appoint commander in chief?"
PICKERING: Colonel Hamilton.

Yet Adams didn't pick Colonel Hamilton. He turned to the sixty-six-year-old ex-President, George Washington, who, it turns out, was so frail that he would die within thirteen months. It's one of history's most fascinating and overlooked subplots. Ex-President George Washington, clad once again in a glittering military uniform, rode on a horse down the capital, reigniting the flames of the Revolution. We have no parallel. Imagine if Dwight Eisenhower, in 1962, once again donned a uniform and oversaw the Vietnam War?

Given Washington's age, everyone knew that his role would be largely ceremonial, and that his number 2, the Inspector General, would have the real clout. Washington refused to accept the commission without Hamilton as his right-hand man, as his loss would be "irreparable." Washington insisted that Hamilton had "the means of viewing everything on a larger scale."

Adams seethed. "If I should consent to the appointment of Hamilton," Adams huffed, "I should consider it as the most irresponsible action of my whole life." Perhaps a bit xenophobic, Adams noted that Hamilton was "not a native of the United States" and that he has "no popular character in any part of America." Adams stuffed this letter in a drawer, never sending it. (Hamilton could learn from this.) Yet he held his nose and gave Hamilton the gig, promoting him to major general.

General Hamilton got to work. Earning just $268.35 a month, he hunkered down to whip up plans for an army and navy, leaving no detail to chance. The huts that the troops would sleep in should be "roofed with boards, unless where slabs can be had very cheap." He asked scientists to help him compute the optimal length for the marching step.

He even recommended Aaron Burr—"Little Burr!" he said with surprising affection—to be one of his brigadier generals. But Washington scotched the idea, noting that "Colonel Burr is a brave and able officer, but the question is whether he has not equal talents at intrigue?"

As part of Burr's "intrigue," in fact, he even hinted that Hamilton should use his army for a coup. "General, you are now at the head of the army," said Aaron Burr. "You are a man of the first talents and vast influence. Our constitution is a miserable paper machine. You have it in your power to demolish it."

"I'm too much troubled with the thing called 'morality,'" Hamilton replied.

"General, all things are moral to great souls!" Burr said, in French.

Hamilton never forgot the conversation. And he must have wondered, how is freaking *Aaron Burr,* of all people, even relevant in politics? Burr had cracked the Top 4 in the Presidential Candidates in 1796, which must have struck Hamilton as preposterous. *Where has this dude been?* Where was Burr at the Constitutional Convention? The Whiskey Rebellion? The Jay Treaty? (Hamilton's rival kept himself busy with at least one task . . . Maria Reynolds eventually divorced her husband, and guess who she hired as her attorney? Aaron Burr. *Muse.*)

General Hamilton focused on his army. After serving for six years in the bloody Revolutionary War, Hamilton had seen, firsthand, the cost in human blood. He had seen soldiers get maimed. So he drew up plans for a military hospital that foreshadowed something like Walter Reed, as "justice and humanity" demanded that we take care of injured soldiers.

His enemies, however, saw the whole army as just more fodder for ridicule, especially in the aftermath of a sex scandal. One tabloid called him "[t]he amorous general." Adams privately referred to him as the "little cock sparrow general," and Jefferson warily called him "our Bonaparte."

That last charge, it must be said, carried a sliver of truth. General Hamilton had grand plans for his army. "Besides eventual security against invasion, we ought certainly to look to the possession of the Floridas and Louisiana and we ought to squint at South America," he suggested, feeding into every tyrannical stereotype. "I do not know whether to laugh or weep," groaned Adams, at a plan Hamilton had endorsed for invading South America, as the "project is as visionary, though far less innocent, than . . . an excursion to the moon in a cart drawn by geese."

Hamilton did more than build the army—he also ramped up the navy. He built ships and put them in action. People forget this, but "the Quasi-War" saw action at sea; by one estimate, over two thousand US merchant ships were taken by the French. Hamilton's navy fought back. Oh, and since there weren't enough navy ships at the time, guess what they used in a pinch? Hamilton's Coast Guard. (Bonus factoid: one of the new navy ships was a schooner called the USS *Enterprise,* giving Hamilton the wispiest of links to Captain Kirk.)

The grand vision for Hamilton's army, of course, would take much longer to manifest. The immediate threat passed, and the "little cock sparrow general" was only able to raise two thousand troops, not the approved ten thousand. Part of it was timing. Adams wrung a surprising peace with France, the crisis faded, and the public lost its appetite for war.

Some historians, it seems, view Hamilton's reign as little more than a curious footnote, an oddity, or even a comical farce. Yet General Hamilton served, at a critical moment, as the head of the United States military. What if we had gone to war with France? Today, we would never mock a general for readying America's troops; it's what you do to keep America safe. In almost any other era of American history, Hamilton's support of the army would be seen as deeply patriotic.

Is it a stretch to call Hamilton the Father of the United States Military? Well, yes; Washington has dibs. But . . . "The military has been in existence since 1798 and therefore was really developed under Hamilton. He was the person to oversee and direct the design, protocol, and structure of the founding of the U.S. Army, U.S. Navy, and U.S. Marines," explains Nicole Scholet de Villavicencio, vice president of the Alexander Hamilton Awareness Society. "He has much more claim to this title than people want to give him, as none of these military branches existed under the U.S. Constitution before Hamilton brought them to life."

General Hamilton also had one more idea. What if America had a military service academy? It should be by the water. It should be in New York. He whipped up plans for the curriculum for the school, which would be called West Point. Finally, he sent Congress "A Bill for Establishing a Military Academy." In yet another irony, in 1802, it would be signed into law by the man who originally opposed it: Thomas Jefferson. Decades later, in 1821, a professor from West Point wrote to Jefferson and thanked him for "the great services you have rendered the nation," as the institution "originated under your patronage." The letter did not mention Hamilton.

JOHN ADAMS'S SALTIEST INSULTS

John Adams was pretty tough on old Hammie, but then again, he ripped every Founding Father. He had the sharpest tongue and the thinnest skin. Some of his fondest words:

JAMES MADISON: "A creature of French puffs. Some of the worst measures, some of the most stupid motions, stand on record to his infamy."

BENJAMIN FRANKLIN: "Jealous and envious . . . False and deceitful . . . His whole life has been one continued insult to good manners and to decency."

THOMAS JEFFERSON: "Instead of being the ardent pursuer of science that some think him, I know he is indolent, and his soul is poisoned."

GEORGE WASHINGTON: "Too illiterate, unlearned, unread, for his station . . . He had derived little knowledge from reading; none from travel, except in the United States." (In other words, Washington should have spent more time traveling, less time winning the Revolutionary War.)

AARON BURR: "Fat as a duck and as ruddy as a roost cock." (This one is especially odd, as Burr was trim and Adams was, well, referred to as "His Rotundity.")

The honor of a collective rebuttal goes to Benjamin Franklin, who described Adams as "always an honest man, often a wise one, and in some things, absolutely out of his senses."

NIP GOSSIP IN THE BUD

—

"I will meet you like a gentleman."

IT'S SIMPLE: IF YOUR COWORKERS are talking trash behind your back, call them out. Confront them directly. Nip the gossip in the bud. (And hopefully your job's HR policy forbids dueling.)

Hamilton had some complicated, hard-to-interpret, and even inconsistent thoughts on dueling. At times he blasted "affairs of honor" as archaic and despicable, noting that "we do not now live in the days of chivalry." Unaware of the dark irony, he once said that if you're trying to prove your own innocence or the "malice of an accuser, the worst method you can take is to run him through the body or shoot him through the head."

One part of Hamilton sided with Benjamin Franklin, who had once asked, "How can such miserable worms as we are entertain so much pride, as to [suppose] that every offense against our imagined honor, merits death?" Franklin penned a quick satire:

A gentleman in a coffee house desired another to sit further from him.

"Why so?"

"Because, Sir, you smell."

"That, Sir, is an affront, and you must fight me."

"I will fight you if you insist, but I don't see how that will mend the matter; for if you kill me, I shall smell too; and if I kill you, you will smell, if possible, more than you do at present."

And yet. Time after time, to protect his good name, Hamilton sprang the threat of a duel. Whenever someone insulted him? If they apologized, great. If not, he suggested they grab pistols.

In 1790, one grumpy congressman gave a speech that dramatically charged, "I give the lie to Colonel Hamilton!" The room was stunned. One senator called it "a violent personal attack . . . which the men of the blade say must produce a duel." It's one thing to attack the treasury secretary's banking plan, it's something else to publicly call him a liar.

Hamilton immediately wrote the congressman and demanded an explanation. Tensions ran high. "The town is much agitated about a duel between Burke and Hamilton," one senator scribbled in his diary. "So many people concerned in the business may really make the fools fight." Once again, after a flurry of letters, the pistols were avoided and Hamilton protected his honor.

A duel also nearly sprang from the Maria Reynolds sex scandal. Furious with James Monroe for leaking the sex receipts ($45 here, $30 there), he told Monroe that "your representation is totally false." *Whoa.* Monroe called Hamilton a "scoundrel." *It's on.*

"I will meet you like a gentleman," wrote Hamilton.

"I am ready, get your pistols," replied the future President.

As always—or nearly always—they settled the matter without bloodshed. The pattern seemed unbreakable. *Insult, threat, resolution.* "Hamilton may have opposed duels on principle, as he later claimed, but for such a hotheaded man these affairs of honor were expedient weapons in silencing his enemies," reasons Chernow. "Whenever he was maligned, Hamilton aggressively sought retractions, persisting to the bitter end."

There's one common thread in all these altercations: Hamilton is the one who initiates the ritual. He is the one who's insulted, he is the one who throws down the gauntlet, he is the one who stakes the moral high ground. At some point he must have wondered . . . what was it like to be on the other side?

DON'T. PRESS. SEND.

—

"[President Adams has an] unfitness for the station."

I N A PARALLEL UNIVERSE, perhaps John Adams and Alexander Hamilton were the best of friends. This would make sense. They agreed on many of the issues, they read the same kinds of books, and they both took a weird delight in thumbing their nose at popular opinion. Both were branded as monarchists. As a lawyer in 1784, Hamilton had courageously defended Tories from the angry New York mob; as a lawyer in 1770, Adams had courageously defended British soldiers during the Boston Massacre. They were the two leading Federalists. They should have been buddies.

They were not buddies. Over the years, Adams had called him "the bastard brat of a Scotch pedlar" and the "Creole bastard." He harped on the immigrant's foreignness: "His place of birth and education were foreign countries; his fortune was poverty itself."

Adams even called the treasury secretary *lazy*. And also a drug user. "I have been told," Adams suggests, "though I cannot vouch for the truth of it . . . that General Hamilton never [spoke] in public without a bit of opium in his mouth." In short, he considered

Alexander Hamilton "the most restless, impatient, artful, indefatigable and unprincipled intriguer in the United States, if not in the world."

As for Hamilton?

He originally liked Adams quite a bit. In 1792, he had praised Adams's "early intrepid, faithful, persevering, and comprehensively useful services to his country." He was right to do so. Let's not forget that in 1776, Adams gave a speech that galvanized Independence Hall and lit the fire of the Revolution—for one shining moment he was, according to Jefferson, the "Atlas of American Independence." Adams is a fun character to root for. "It's impossible not to love John Adams," gushes Brookhiser, noting that his blunt humor "strikes us as a blast of fresh air." Then again, "none of these traits prepared him to be a good president."

And there's the rub. In the four acidic years of the Adams administration, a wary truce devolved into an open feud. Hamilton thought Adams to be incompetent; Adams viewed Hamilton as meddling.

Then came the Quasi-War. While General Hamilton trained his army for a war with France, President Adams, in secret, and without consulting his cabinet, negotiated a peace treaty with Paris. Maybe that could have been the end of it.

Yet both men were too combustible. Adams finally canned his cabinet—okay, fair enough—but then he called it a "British faction" that was secretly controlled by Hamilton.

"British" was still a dirty word. A fighting word. It came close to accusing someone of treason. Hamilton, of course, couldn't leave that insult alone. (Nip gossip in the bud.) He wrote Adams— *the sitting US President*—a letter filled with coded language that could trigger a duel. "I must, sir, take it for granted that you cannot have made such assertions or insinuations without being willing to avow them."

The President never replied.

A month later he wrote the President a second time, calling the insult "a base, wicked, and cruel calumny, destitute even of a plausible pretext."

The President never replied.

What could Hamilton do? What he always did: write. So he dropped another manifesto with another punchy title: "Letter from Alexander Hamilton, Concerning the Public Conduct and Character of John Adams, Esq., President of the United States."

The letter wasn't intended for the masses. Hamilton only thought that two hundred bigwigs in the Federalist Party, give or take, would see this damning treatise. But someone got ahold of the letter and reproduced it widely—many historians think it was Aaron Burr.

The fifty-four-page pamphlet savagely attacked the President. Hamilton conceded that Adams had "patriotism and integrity, and even talents of a certain kind," but mocked his "defects of character" and "extreme egotism." He charged that Adams had "a vanity without bounds and a jealousy capable of discoloring every object."

Most damning: he had "unfitness for the station" of the presidency.

It was the Reynolds pamphlet all over again. One Federalist noted that the pamphlet is "new proof that you are a *dangerous man.*" His nineteenth-century biographer Henry Cabot Lodge called it "a piece of passionate folly . . . simple madness."

Even Robert Troup, one of Hamilton's lifelong friends, said that there's "not a man in the whole circle of our friends who but condemns it."

The Republicans must have popped champagne. As Madison wrote Jefferson, "I rejoice with you that Republicanism is likely to be so *completely* triumphant."

Hamilton was seemingly oblivious. At this point sounding out of touch, he even asked friends for "new anecdotes" about a possible second edition. (His friends talked him out of it.)

I am not going to dignify this with a response! is something of a cliché in politics. But in 1800 that really did apply. President Adams, wisely, never bothered with a response, noting that "I am confident it will do more harm than me." Adams was right. And he had the last laugh. Whereas Hamilton would soon grab his pistols for an early-morning duel, John Adams would have another twenty-six years to tell his side of the story. (This is yet another reason that we never heard much about Hamilton in grade school.) The other victim here? The Federalist Party. No Federalist was ever again elected President.

Hamilton's great-great-great-great-great-grandson, Douglas Hamilton, still looks at this moment with horror. "Don't press Send!" he says. "I think a lot about this when working with clients. Maybe I have something angry to say, then I'll type the email, then I don't press Send. Later I'm glad that I didn't."

For better or worse—and increasingly worse—Alexander Hamilton always pressed Send.

10
HONOR

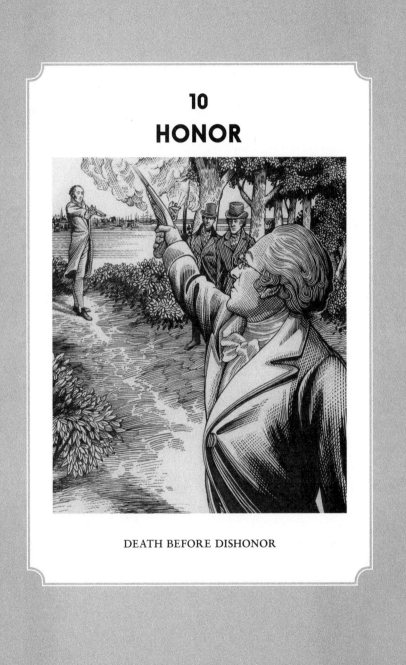

DEATH BEFORE DISHONOR

NEVER BREAK A PROMISE
(EVEN A TINY ONE)
—

"A promise must never be broken."

WHEN YOU MAKE A PROMISE, big or small, you keep it. No matter what. As a student at King's College, Hamilton once misplaced some documents and, without prompting, felt compelled to write the owner: "It is with the utmost chagrin I am obliged to inform you, that I am not able to return you all your pamphlets; and what is still worse the most valuable of them is missing." He's like the myth of George Washington and the cherry tree—"I cannot tell a lie."

Even his opponents acknowledged Hamilton's unbending integrity. One political rival once admitted that "on his word I could rely equally as his oath." Thomas Jefferson agreed, describing Hamilton as "a singular character" who is "honest . . . and honorable in all transactions, amiable in society, and duly valuing virtue in public life."

Consider a letter he wrote to his oldest and most beloved son, Philip, when the nine-year-old was away at school. First he tells his son:

> *Your mamma and myself were very happy to learn that you are pleased with your situation,*

He then congratulates Philip on doing a good job in class, as the kid is clearly bright, quick, and a budding young orator.

> *Your master also informs me that you recited a lesson the first day you began, very much to his satisfaction.*

Next, Hamilton can't pass up a chance to remind his son of the value of hard work:

> *I am sure you have too much spirit not to exert yourself that you may make us every day more and more proud of you.*

Lest Philip start coasting on his homework, Hamilton says:

> *I expect every letter from [the schoolmaster] will give me a fresh proof of your progress, for I know you can do a great deal if you please.*

Then he gets to the promise. Just as millions of parents email their kids at college to ask about their plans for winter break, Hamilton needs to coordinate the next visit with his son:

> *You remember that I engaged to send for you next Saturday, and I will do it, unless you request me to put it off, for*

a promise must never be broken, and I never will make you one, which I will not fulfill as far as I am able . . .

He reminds Philip that he made him a promise, and he's not one to go back on his word. But . . .

but it has occurred to me that the Christmas holidays are near at hand, and I suppose your school will then break up for a few days and give you an opportunity of coming to stay with us for a longer time than if you should come on Saturday.

On the one hand this letter is so trivial, so mundane. Yet it gets to the core of his character. It would have been easy for Hamilton to say something like, "You know what? Kid, you should come home over Christmas, as that would give us more time together."

Instead, he views his original commitment—*let's hang out on Saturday*—as a binding covenant. Hamilton made a promise; he will keep it. So he puts the power in the hands of his nine-year-old son, asking him:

Will it not be best, therefore, to put off your journey till the holidays? But determine as you like best, and let me know what will be most pleasing to you. A good night to my darling son.

Throughout his life, in every context, Hamilton shows a near-fanatical respect for integrity. (There is, of course, one glaring exception, but even with the Maria Reynolds affair, Hamilton took a stubborn pride in telling the truth.) Yet is there such a thing as being "too truthful"? Is it possible that concern for your honor—a slavish adherence to a promise—can hurt yourself or the ones you love?

TEACH A MORAL CODE

—

"What can I do better than withdraw from the scene? Every day proves to me more and more, that this American world was not made for me."

L ET'S KEEP OUR FOCUS on young Philip. By 1801, the "flower of the family" had turned nineteen and graduated from Columbia, with honors. Philip was a courteous kid, who, like his father, charmed the adults. In one letter he thanks his grandfather (Philip Schuyler) for advice that he would need to follow "in order to be a good man."

He even had his father's swagger, as one day he gave a speech at Columbia, but was dismayed that the president of the university had cut the sentence that, in Philip's opinion, was "the best and most animated." (The sentence in question: "Americans, you have fought the battles of mankind, you have enkindled that sacred fire of freedom.")

Philip was handsome, quick-witted, and also had Alexander's gift with the ladies. Remembering what it was like to be nineteen in New York City, his father called him a "naughty young man."

On a break from studies one afternoon, Philip and a buddy went to go see a play called, oddly enough, *The West-Indian.*

They noticed a political ally of Jefferson, George Eacker, seated in the next box. Philip knew Eacker and he didn't like him. A few months earlier, Eacker had given a speech that had accused Hamilton of using his army against the Republicans.

So Philip, being a hotheaded nineteen-year-old, confronted Eacker and called him out. The men argued. Then Eacker did the unthinkable and called Philip a *"rascal."* Uh-oh. That's NC-17 language. "Rascal" was one of the foulest, raunchiest insults of the eighteenth century. (Another one just as bad: "Puppy.")

"Who do you call damned rascals?" the teenagers charged back.

The two men nearly got in a fistfight, right there in the lobby of the theater. As they were pulled apart and Eacker returned to his seats, he called to the teenagers, "I shall expect to hear from you."

"You shall," they called back.

It was *on.* "I shall expect to hear from you," of course, was the polite way to say, "Let's get the damn pistols." At this point Philip couldn't back down. If society knew that he shirked the word "rascal," he would have no political future and no personal honor. Philip learned this from his father.

Hamilton advised Philip on how to proceed, stressing his moral code. He despised the act of dueling, and on moral grounds, he thought that shooting your opponent would count as murder. Yet personal honor must be defended. There were no good options. You're either a murderer or a coward. So Hamilton suggested that his son follow Secret Option C: a move the French called the *delope.*

Basically, a *delope* means that you throw away your shot. You either fire at a tree or you don't fire at all. "The *deloper* had to let the other man fire at him first, giving no hint of what he was planning to do," explains Thomas Fleming, author of *Duel*. "If the other man insisted on another shot, he could be accused of being bloodthirsty." This would end the duel right there. Others had used this strategy successfully. The prime minister of England, for example, had recently employed the *delope,* no one was hurt, and he emerged a hero.

This was a high-stakes game of chicken. It's critical to remember that in the majority of cases, no one died in a duel. (One study showed that even when the men grabbed pistols, 80 percent of duels ended without death.) Often the duels were concluded before anyone fired a single shot, and then, *if* shots fired—and no one died—a second round of negotiations would begin.

Eacker had actually challenged *both* of the teenagers to a duel. Philip's friend went first. They fired four shots. No one was hurt. The matter was closed.

The next day it was Philip's turn. At three o'clock in the afternoon on November 22, 1801, the teenager met Eacker on the shores of Weehawken, New Jersey. He borrowed pistols from his uncle, Angelica's husband.

Philip counted his paces. He turned to stare at his opponent. Eacker raised his pistol. And with the idea of honor ringing in his head, and his father's advice guiding his actions, Philip refused to fire.

Eacker, however, shot to kill.

The bullet struck Phillip just above the hip. The young man collapsed to the ground, gushed blood, and was quickly rowed back across the Hudson River. A doctor and Hamilton rushed to his side. One of Hamilton's college friends described the devastating scene: "On a bed without curtains lay poor Phil, pale and languid, his rolling, distorted eyeballs darting forth the flashes of delirium—on one side of him on the same bed—lay his agonized father—on the other side his distracted mother."

Within a day he was dead.

"Never did I see a man so completely overwhelmed with grief," a friend said of Hamilton, who had lost his mother at the age of eleven, and now, at the age of forty-four, lost his son. The ache would haunt the final chapter of his life. "What can I do better than withdraw from the scene?" he asked. "Every day proves to me more and more, that this American world was not made for me."

Philip's death would shadow the Hamilton family for nearly a century. The oldest daughter, Angelica (named for Eliza's sister), had a mental breakdown and went insane, speaking about her dead brother for years, then decades, as if he were still alive. Even as a seventy-three-year-old in 1856, she still asked about her dear brother.

What is the price of honor? This is not a simple question or answer. And we can't be too quick to judge Hamilton by today's standards. At first blush, Hamilton's counsel does seem like spectacularly bad parenting advice. "Killing men in duels was immoral, though dueling, it seems, was not. This was terrible advice to have given," writes Brookhiser in an unsparing critique. "[Hamilton's own father] had been a bad father and an irresponsible man, yet he had never given lethal advice to his sons. How much better a father, for all his solicitude, had Alexander been?"

Brutal. Yet possibly unfair. First, it's unclear that Hamilton knew his son was *actually* going to set foot on the dueling grounds, as opposed to just negotiate the terms over letters. (According to one account, Hamilton went searching for his son and when he learned that Philip was dueling, he fainted in shock.)

Second, the context matters. "This was the culture. Honor was the most important currency you owned, and your whole worth was based around it," argues Nicole Scholet de Villavicencio. "You would not be respected by anyone if you didn't face a duel. Would it have been good parenting advice to encourage your son to murder someone instead? If anything, the fact that Hamilton stood for a moral code within the social protocol should be lauded."

That, then, is the takeaway: Hamilton stood for a moral code, and he imparted this code to his children. The question of what to do in a clash between *morality* and *practicality*, of course, has enthralled philosophers since the days of Plato, Socrates, and Ned Stark. It's not an easy call, and perhaps Hamilton felt guilty. Perhaps he wished that it was he, not his son, who had stared down a bullet on the shores of Weehawken. He would soon have that chance.

WHAT IF BURR HAD MISSED?

Thomas Fleming, the author of *Duel,* imagines the ultimate counterfactual: What if Burr had missed?

The divergence starts in 1808. "Historians have been reluctant to admit the full dimensions of Jefferson's disastrous second term," writes Fleming, noting that when the French and British attacked US merchant ships, instead of responding with force— what Hamilton would have done—President Jefferson placed an embargo on all trade, which crippled the US economy.

If he'd been alive, argues Fleming, Hamilton would have used this issue to mount a political comeback, winning the White House. President Hamilton then would have beefed up the military and won the War of 1812, "making Canada part of the United States."

President Hamilton would have created technical schools in every state, dug more canals, and spurred faster adoption of the steam engine. The nation would have gotten even richer. Soon it would have gobbled up Florida, Texas, and possibly Mexico, eventually absorbing much of South America. Now enormously popular, President Hamilton would have "refused to retire after two terms," which, frankly, seems plausible, as he'd urged Washington to stay for a third.

"Finally, President Hamilton would have tackled the greatest problem America ever faced: slavery," suggests Fleming, passing a constitutional amendment that would phase out slavery over twenty-five years, giving the South time to adjust economically. "Hamilton remained in office for twenty-two years, dying in the White House in 1830." There would have never been a Civil War.

ALWAYS FAITHFUL

—

"The wounded heart derives a degree of consolation from the tenderness with which its loss is bewailed by the virtuous, the wise, and humane."

—ELIZA HAMILTON

HAMILTON WAS A MODEL of faithfulness, fidelity, and honor in every single aspect of life. And by Hamilton, of course, here we mean Eliza Hamilton.

History will never know the exact details of how she reacted to the Maria Reynolds scandal. Did they fight? Have a shouting match? Did Hamilton sleep on the couch? As the musical points out, Eliza burned every single one of her letters, so we can only guess at her side of the story. (Context: It is not, however, a given that she burned those letters in anger. Burning letters was actually not that uncommon—sort of a Revolutionary-era version of formatting a hard drive. Even Martha Washington burned her letters to George.)

Yet this is what we do know. In the years and decades after Hamilton's death, Eliza fought to honor his legacy, she remained faithful, and she spoke frequently of their love. Every scrap of evidence casts her as a woman of strength, loyalty, and forgiveness.

Remember those poems that Hamilton had written Eliza to charm and court her, many years ago? (*No joy unmixed my bosom warms . . . But when my angel's in my arms.*) She kept them. She treasured them. The paper began to yellow and fray, but Eliza stitched the parchment together and wore these poems, in a small bag, on a necklace. She later described Hamilton as "my beloved, sainted husband and my guardian angel."

True, she was wounded by the affair. She must have been. "Whatever pain she suffered, however, Eliza never surrendered her conviction that her husband was a noble patriot who deserved the veneration of his countrymen and had been crucified by a nefarious band," writes Chernow. "Her later work for orphans, the decades spent compiling her husband's papers and supervising his biography, her constant delight in talking about him, her pride in Washington's wine cooler, her fight to stake Hamilton's claim to authorship of the farewell address—these and many, many other things testify to unflinching love for her husband."

The Hamilton marriage, after being tested and bruised and even mocked in the press, seems, somehow, to have survived and even grown stronger. Hamilton's later letters suggest a love that has deepened, matured:

> *You are my good genius of that kind which the ancient philosophers called a <u>familiar</u> and you know very well that I am glad to be in every way as familiar as possible with you.*

He seems to now fully grasp the towering strength of his "familiar," writing:

I am much more in debt to you than I can ever pay, but my future life will be more than ever devoted to your happiness.

Together they built a new home, in present-day Harlem, that they called the Grange, as a nod to Hamilton's Scottish ancestral home. The home is still standing, with place settings at the dinner table. (You can walk on the same original floorboards as Eliza and Alexander Hamilton.)

As a family, the Hamiltons planted flowers and apple trees. "There should be nine of each sort of flowers," Hamilton suggested to Eliza. "They may be arranged thus: wild roses around the outside of the flower garden with laurel at foot." They worked together on a garden, swapping plans for the white pines and the tulip trees. ("A few dogwood trees, not large, scattered along the margin of the grove would be very pleasant.")

After her husband's death, Eliza showcased her own Hamiltonian energy and attention to detail, spearheading the launch of New York's first private orphanage, managing the project, and crunching the numbers and mastering the finances.

One son described her as "remarkable for sprightliness and vivacity," while another son noted that "she was a most earnest, energetic, and intelligent woman."

"Mamma, you are a sturdy beggar," her son once told her, referring to her tireless fundraising efforts.

"I cannot spare myself or others," she replied. "My Maker has pointed out this duty to me and has given me the ability and inclination to perform it."

Eliza later moved to D.C., where she led the movement to raise money for the Washington Monument, along with Dolley Madison. She met generations of US Presidents—as late as Millard Fillmore in 1853.

She lived to be ninety-seven, faithful till the end.

CHARACTER FIRST
—

"[Aaron Burr] is one of the worst sort—a friend to
nothing but as it suits his interest and ambition."

L ET'S BACK UP JUST A BIT. Before Hamilton suffered the
pangs of Philip's death, he took center stage in the
carnival-like election of 1800.

With roughly half the nation Federalist and half the
nation Republican, in an odd quirk of the electoral map, whoever
won New York State would win the election. And the state, in
turn, would go to whoever won New York City. The fate of the
nation, quite literally, hinged on the action below 14th Street. (It's
every smug Manhattanite's fantasy.)

Aaron Burr campaigned for the Republicans, Hamilton for
the Federalists. They rode on horseback to crisscross Manhattan, rounding up supporters and giving speeches. "Every day he is
seen in the streets," one newspaper wrote of Hamilton, "hurrying
this way, darting that." Sometimes they gave dueling speeches on
the same corner.

The forty-three-year-old hustled the streets from dawn to
dusk, summoning a young man's energy. He recruited his longtime friends for the cause, such as Robert Troup, who complained

that "I have not eaten dinner for three days, and have been constantly upon my legs from 7 in the morning till 7 in the afternoon." (One historian called Troup an "overworked fat man.")

It was the nation's first true political campaign. And Burr was better at it. While Hamilton might have had the clarity to envision a modern-day American economy, Burr had the clarity to envision modern-day American politics. He kept files on each voter with personalized notes, he targeted the city's German voters with German-speaking volunteers, and he sliced and diced the electorate with a twenty-first-century savvy.

Burr turned his own home into America's first political war room. It operated 24/7, offered free coffee, and even had mattresses for exhausted staffers. Aaron Burr had found his calling: the sport of politics offered him "a great deal of fun."

Burr scanned the list of voters and shrewdly made a plan for each. "Ask nothing of this one," he advised. "If we demand money, he'll be offended and refuse to work for us . . . Double this man's assessment. He'll contribute generously if he doesn't have to work." One local congressman remembered that Burr attended the polling places "for 24 hours without sleeping or resting."

He had more tricks up his sleeve. Burr organized a fleet of "carriages, chairs and wagons" to boost voter turnout. In modern parlance, Burr had the better ground game. When it came to campaigning, as one onlooker observed, Burr was "as superior to the Hamiltonians as a man is to a boy." Hamilton was out of his element. The way you won arguments, in Hamilton's mind, was by starting at the foundational truths, following the chain of logic, and then sharing the conclusions.

Yet that is not how you win elections.

Burr won in a landslide. As he gloated to one Federalist, "We have beat you by superior *Management*."

Clarification: *Both* Jefferson and Burr were running against John Adams. Burr did not campaign against Jefferson. (It's a weedy nuance that, understandably, is condensed in the musical.) By securing New York City for the Republicans, Burr had assured a defeat of the Federalists and, theoretically, handed the White House to Thomas Jefferson, with him getting Veep as a thank-you present.

Yet this is not how it played out.

It's worth remembering that back then, as the rules stated, if you were running for President, then you didn't have a running mate—you were stuck with the guy who came in second. The party leaders found a workaround. For the first two elections, the party leaders had carefully choreographed the voting so that Washington would get the most votes, then Adams. (Guess who masterminded this? Hamilton nudged a few Federalists to with-hold their votes for Adams—not out of spite, but to ensure that the election wouldn't end in a tie.)

Jefferson and the Republicans flubbed the math. Clearly the plan called for Jefferson to have the most votes, then Burr. But the Republicans didn't have a Hamilton to calibrate the votes. It ended in a tie—73 for Jefferson, 73 for Burr. To the Republicans this was a clerical error, a technicality. *The plan was Jefferson 1st, Burr 2nd*. Everyone expected Burr to step down.

But he did not.

So this "tie" was thrown into the House, which, at the time, was still controlled by the lame-duck Federalists. This gave them a juicy opportunity. Burr had flirted with the Federalist Party before; perhaps he'd become one of them after all?

The House voted—it ended in a tie.

So they voted a second time—also a tie.

They voted a third time. Fourth. Fifth. The House voted *thirty-five* times, making the "hanging chads" recount of 2000 look like democracy's Platonic Form.

Enter Alexander Hamilton.

By now, General Hamilton must have seen Aaron Burr as the opposite of everything he believed in. He charged that Burr "[has] no principle, public or private . . . and will listen to no monitor but his ambition." He added that "in civil life, he has never projected nor aided in producing a single measure of important public utility."

Hamilton dispatched letter after letter to the Federalists, warning them of Burr's lack of character. "As to Burr, there is nothing in his favor. His private character is not defended by his most partial friends. He is bankrupt beyond redemption, except by the plunder of his country."

He kept going. "His public principles have no other spring or aim than his own aggrandizement . . . If he can, he will certainly disturb our institutions to secure to himself *permanent power* and with it *wealth*." The attacks continued. "As a public man . . . [Burr] is one of the worst sort—a friend to nothing but as it suits his interest and ambition."

Jefferson himself would agree with Hamilton. "I never indeed thought him an honest, frank-dealing man," Jefferson later said.

"But considered him as a crooked gun or other perverted machine, whose aim or shot you could never be sure of."

Jefferson or Burr? Hamilton plainly addressed the choice.

"If there be a man in the world I ought to hate," Hamilton admitted, "it is Jefferson. With Burr I have always been personally well." Yet Jefferson "is by far not so dangerous a man and he has pretensions to character . . . [Burr] is far more cunning than wise, far more dexterous than able. In my opinion he is inferior in real ability to Jefferson."

Hamilton doubled down on his critique of Burr, telling a friend that he is "one of the worst men in the community. The appointment of Burr as president would disgrace our country abroad . . . No agreement with him could be relied upon . . . He is sanguine enough to hope every thing, daring enough to attempt everything, but enough to scruple nothing." If Federalists backed Burr, they would be "signing their own death warrant." Hamilton felt it "a religious duty to oppose his career."

In other words: #NeverBurr.

At last, and possibly influenced by Hamilton's letters (historians debate this), a few Federalists switched their votes and Jefferson won the White House. Burr did indeed claim the vice presidency, but he found himself marginalized by Jefferson, who felt betrayed by all the shenanigans. Burr seethed for the next four years.

Meanwhile, General Hamilton tried to focus on Eliza, the kids, his legal practice, and his new home in Harlem. He was broke. He wrote a client in 1802 that it "would be amazingly convenient to me to touch your money as soon as possible." (This is a far cry from the brazen twentysomething who had shrugged off payment.) After Philip's death he said that a "gloom hangs over my mind." His financial ledgers include a devastating entry: "1802 - May 12 - Expenses Philip's funeral - 266.11."

Perhaps to distract himself from the grief, he spent more time in his and Eliza's new garden. He soon found that gardening, apparently, was one of the few things that he did not do well. (He told a friend that "the greatest part of my little farm will be devoted to grass.") Sensing himself in the twilight of his political life, he called gardening the "usual refugee of a disappointed politician," and noted that he was "as little fitted" to be a farmer "as Jefferson to guide the helm of the United States."

Flash-forward to 1804. Hamilton was stirred from his garden by news that Burr, dumped from the ticket in Jefferson's second term, was now running for governor of New York. Hamilton heard whispers, in fact, that Burr was secretly meeting with Federalists about organizing a plot to have New York secede from the Union. This was more than mere gossip. Upstate New Yorkers, furious with Jefferson and Virginia, thought about forming their own nation . . . with Aaron Burr to lead them.

Hamilton left his garden.

For one final time, Hamilton jumped back to the fray. Once again Hamilton urged the Federalists to oppose Aaron Burr. Once again Burr lost the election. At a dinner party, he denounced Burr as "dangerous," and, according to one witness at the party, Hamilton expressed a "still more despicable opinion" of Aaron Burr.

Still more despicable . . .

Normally that wouldn't be a big deal. Hamilton had said far worse, after all. It had never caused a problem.

But this time something was different. A newspaper picked up the story. The words "dangerous . . . still more despicable" made their way into print.

Aaron Burr read this newspaper. He must have read the article a second time, a third. His honor had been insulted. Publicly. So he took a page from Hamilton's own playbook: he would nip the gossip in the bud.

DEATH BEFORE DISHONOR

—

"You had rather I should die innocent than live guilty."

BURR THOUGHT ABOUT THE WORDS *"still more despicable opinion. . . ."* He must have thought about how he had just lost the election of 1804, thanks to Hamilton. How he had lost the election of 1800, thanks to Hamilton. And perhaps he thought about how, in 1776, he was booted from Washington's inner circle . . . maybe thanks to Hamilton?

Enough.

Or, in another interpretation, perhaps Burr simply viewed this as a way to launch a political comeback. "There is no deep, dark, mysterious insult at the heart of the Burr-Hamilton duel," writes Joanne Freeman. "Like any other politician, Burr was manipulating the code of honor to redeem his reputation after the humiliation of a lost election, seizing on this insult above others because it was in writing, vague as it might be."

Whatever the true motivations, Burr sent a letter to Hamilton's downtown law office at 12 Garden Street:

Sir,

*I send for your perusal a letter signed Ch. Dr. Cooper . . .
You might perceive, Sir, the necessity of a prompt and un-
qualified acknowledgement or denial of the use of any
expressions which could warrant the assertions of Dr.
Cooper.*

I have the honor to be Your Obt Svt

A. Burr

Hamilton read the letter carefully. He then read the attached
newspaper clipping, which he might have been reading for the
first time. *"A still more despicable opinion . . ."*

(To quickly connect the dots: "Dr. Cooper" was at the dinner
party where Hamilton had said the words "of a still more despicable opinion." He's the witness who fed it to the newspaper.)

General Hamilton was puzzled. What was Burr asking him to
disavow, exactly? As Fleming explains, "The language of insult
between gentlemen usually required a specific term, unmistak-
ably from the lips of the insulter, such as *rascal, liar, scoundrel,*
to bring things to the brink of gunfire." So Hamilton asked Burr
to get more specific.

Sir,

*I have maturely reflected on the subject of your letter . . .
and the more I have reflected the more I have become convinced, that I could not, without manifest impropriety,
make the avowal or disavowal which you seem to think
necessary.*

He then—and this would be funny, if it were not deadly—gives Burr something of a grammar lesson.

> *The phrase "still more despicable" admits of infinite shades, from very light to very dark. How am I to judge of the degree intended? Or how shall I annex any precise idea to language so indefinite? Between Gentlemen, <u>despicable</u> and <u>more despicable</u> are not worth the pains of a distinction.*
>
> . . .
>
> *I have the honor to be Sir Your obed. servt*
>
> A Hamilton

Burr was not amused. He found the letter to be pedantic and mocking.

> *Sir,*
>
> *Your letter of the 20th has been this day received. Having considered it attentively I regret to find in it nothing of that sincerity and delicacy which you profess to value.*

Then Burr gets to the guts of it, reminding Hamilton of "the necessity of a rigid adherence to the laws of honor and the rule of decorum."

Burr had just played the Honor Card.

According to the vice president, the question did not rest on whether Dr. Cooper:

> *. . . has understood the meaning of the word [despicable] or has used it according to syntax and with grammatical accuracy, but whether you have authorized this*

application either directly or by uttering expressions or
opinions derogatory to my honor . . .

　Your letter has furnished me with new reasons for re-
quiring a definite reply.

　I have the honor to be sir your obt st

A. Burr

Burr then tells Hamilton, "No denial or declaration will be
satisfactory unless it be *general.*"

For Hamilton that would be impossible. How could he make
a "general" declaration that he had never, in fifteen years, said
anything insulting? He viewed that as too open-ended.

Sir,

Your first letter, in a style too peremptory, made a demand,
in my opinion, unprecedented and unwarrantable. My an-
swer, pointing out the embarrassment, gave you an oppor-
tunity to take a less exceptional course.

　. . .

　I have no other answer to give than that which has al-
ready been given.

　. . .

　I have the honor to be Sir Your obed servt.

A Hamilton

And that was that.

What was Hamilton really thinking? For over two hundred
years, historians have debated his true motivations and they will
do so for the next two hundred. Some have speculated that he
had a death wish and wanted to die as a martyr. ("I have no other

wish than as soon as possible to make a brilliant exit," he wrote to John Laurens during the Revolutionary War. " 'Tis a weakness, but I feel I am not fit for this terrestrial country.")

A few have even suggested that General Hamilton had, himself, hoped to take command of a secessionist army that would split from the Union. (Brookhiser debunks these conspiracy theories, calling it "an unlikely ambition for a man who had put down two rebellions in Pennsylvania and who despised the revolution in France: one revolution had been enough for his lifetime.") Hamilton had spent his entire adult life defending the Union. He was no secessionist.

Another theory is that, for pragmatic reasons, Hamilton still had further military ambitions. That's less far-fetched. Hamilton had effectively retired from *politics*. He had not, however, retired from the public. There's a subtle difference. If a war came, he would be the rightful heir to lead the military. (War with France was still a possibility, as the unpredictable Napoléon still glowered from across the ocean.) And only eight years later, of course, would come the War of 1812. In a parallel universe, it's a good bet that General Hamilton, who would have been only fifty-five, would have commanded the army. None of that could happen if he had shirked a duel.

Hamilton had yet one more motivation for dueling Burr: *to prevent Burr from committing treason*. He could do this even in death. In one of his final letters, Hamilton said that he accepted the duel for "the ability to be in the future useful . . . whether in resisting mischief or in effecting good." The night before the duel, in the very last letter he sent, the general warned of the "dismemberment of our empire." It was clearly top of mind.

If Hamilton refused to duel, he would be branded a coward and lose every last drop of political juice, opening the door for a President Burr at the head of a northern confederacy. From this perspective, Hamilton's motivation was to literally save the Union. "As odd as it seems, Hamilton needed to face Burr in order to preserve his reputation because without his reputation and his honor, he could no longer serve his country," explains historian William Chrystal. "In the final analysis, Alexander Hamilton faced Aaron Burr for the people of the United States of America. It was his final sacrifice for his country."

Thankfully, we do have one primary source to give us a glimpse into his motivation for the duel: Hamilton himself. He wrote a letter that walked through his logic.

Hamilton first acknowledged that, yes, of course, he was "certainly desirous of avoiding this interview." He gives four reasons why he should *decline* the duel:

1) His "religious and moral principles" disallowed dueling. Hamilton had become more religious since his son's death.
2) He would be leaving Eliza and the kids behind.
3) He would be leaving a financial debt. (He had skimped on the life insurance.)
4) He said he was not aware of any ill will to Colonel Burr.

All of these arguments, agreed Hamilton, were ample reason to avoid the duel. But. There remains a nagging truth: he really did say despicable things about Burr. His honor would not let him recant. That would be a lie. And Alexander Hamilton didn't lie.

Furthermore, if he denied these statements, then he would

effectively be calling the *original source* of these insults (Dr. Cooper, the guy from the newspaper clipping) a liar, which, in addition to being dishonorable, could trigger yet another duel— putting him back to square one. The truth was the truth. The core of Hamilton's character had never changed; as a clerk on St. Croix, when only twelve years old, he had written his friend Neddy that he would "willingly *risk my life tho' not my character* to exalt my station."

But. He also had a moral objection to killing a man.

There was only one way out of this logical cul-de-sac: just like he had advised his son Philip, and in a stunning departure from the musical's catchiest line, Alexander Hamilton would throw away his shot. "I have resolved," Hamilton explained, "if our interview is conducted in the usual manner, and it pleases God to give me the opportunity, to *reserve* and *throw away* my first fire."

Hamilton's good friend and right-hand man for the duel (his "second"), Nathaniel Pendleton, thought this was madness. Pendleton argued that firing at Burr, surely, would count as self-defense. His friend Rufus King said the same thing. King argued that if Hamilton was going to actually take the field, then "he owed it to his family and the rights of self defense" to return fire.

At first this seems puzzling. "The fifth commandment, Thou Shalt Not Kill, does not prohibit a Christian from self-defense," writes a befuddled Fleming. "This sudden dread of taking the life of another was also totally at variance with the General's stated readiness to take command of the American army in the event of a war, in which, presumably, he would kill a great many people."

Yet this course of action, which looks so irrational to modern eyes, lets Hamilton thread the needle and protect his honor, his legacy, and the nation itself. "He had satisfied the code of honor by accepting Burr's challenge, violating civil law only under duress," explains Joanne Freeman. "He had maintained his political integrity by refusing to apologize for sincere political convictions. Now he would uphold his moral and religious principles by withholding his fire." And again, others had successfully pulled this off—in 1798, the prime minister of England, when dueling a member of Parliament, used this exact strategy.

The die was cast. Soon the seconds arranged the details.

When: Two weeks' time.

Where: Weehawken, New Jersey. The exact spot where Philip was killed.

How: Using the exact same pistols held by Philip.

In his remaining days the general spent time with Eliza and the children, tied up the loose ends of ongoing legal cases, and composed his will—somehow convincing himself, through optimistic math, that he was leaving Eliza a surplus. (He wasn't.)

Friends remembered that he seemed in good spirits. He attended a Fourth of July dinner of Revolutionary War veterans where, after sitting next to Aaron Burr, he climbed onto the table and sang:

'Twas in the merry month of May
When bees from flower to flower did hum,
Soldiers through the town marched gay,
The village flew to the sound of the drum.

. . .

> *"We're going to war, and when we die*
> *We'll want a man of God nearby,*
> *So bring your Bible and follow the drum."*

Aaron Burr did not sing. The room of grown men and war veterans, who did not know about the duel, had tears in their eyes. Then Hamilton composed one final letter to Eliza:

> *This letter, my dear Eliza, will not be delivered to you, unless I shall first have terminated my earthly career; to begin, as I humbly hope from redeeming grace and divine mercy, a happy immortality.*

"A happy immortality" is certainly putting a positive spin on things. He again walks through the stubborn logic that Eliza must have found maddening:

> *If it had been possible for me to have avoided the interview, my love for you and my precious children would have been alone a decisive motive. But it was not possible, without sacrifices which would have rendered me unworthy of your esteem . . . The consolations of Religion, my beloved, can alone support you; and these you have a right to enjoy. Fly to the bosom of your God and be comforted. With my last idea; I shall cherish the sweet hope of meeting you in a better world.*
>
> *Adieu best of wives and best of Women. Embrace all my darling children for me.*
>
> *Ever yours*
AH.

And then it was almost time.

On July 11, 1804, the general left his home at 5 a.m. The sky was still dark. He headed to the docks of present-day Greenwich Village, crossing the same streets where, years ago, he had lugged artillery and fought the British. He climbed into a small boat. Then he pushed off from the docks with his second, Pendleton, a few oarsmen, and the physician Dr. Hosack.

The men rowed. In the quiet of the early morning, Hamilton looked back at Manhattan, the growing mecca that he had helped create, and said, "It's going to be a great city someday."

They reached Weehawken at dawn. Hamilton took in the sight of a grassy ledge and a large boulder. He walked on, or very near, the same dirt where his son had been killed. The sun peeked above the ridge, low enough to strike the river at an angle that caused a glare.

They tossed a coin to see who would pick the positions. Hamilton won. They then tossed a coin to see who would give the command to fire. Hamilton won again. Perhaps he thought his luck would continue.

The seconds loaded the pistols.

"Do you want the hairspring trigger set?" Pendleton asked.

"Not this time," replied Hamilton, which was odd, as this was his first duel.

The seconds then walked through the rules. When Pendleton yelled out "Present!" they had the green light to fire.

Hamilton asked for a moment's pause, looked at the sunlight, and then put on his glasses. (Another detail that historians have debated for centuries—did the glasses mean that Hamilton was aiming to kill? Or aiming *not* to kill?)

The general and the vice president both settled into the duelist stance—right foot in front of the left, body at an angle, keeping a slim profile. They sucked in their stomachs.

They stared at each other. Waited for the command. And finally it was time.

"Present!"

Gunshots.

HONOR YOUR COUNTRY

—

"If they break this union, they will break my heart."

T HIS IS A MORTAL WOUND, DOCTOR."

Bleeding, in agony, Hamilton remained calm as the others scrambled in horror. "Take care of that pistol," Hamilton warned them, somehow speaking through the pain. "It may go off and do harm."

Hamilton lost all feeling of his legs. He drifted in and out of consciousness. They rowed him back across the Hudson River and rushed him to a friend's house in Lower Manhattan, on Jane Street, carrying his body on a cot. News of the duel began to ricochet through the city. Someone posted a bulletin at Tontine Coffee House that blared: "General Hamilton was shot by Colonel Burr this morning in a duel. The General is said to be mortally wounded." Manhattan began to weep. "All business seemed to be suspended in the city," wrote one contemporary, as "a solemn gloom hangs on every countenance."

Eliza rushed from the Grange and hovered over his bed, in tears, devastated. She must have been shocked—just yesterday he was calmly at home composing letters. Hamilton tried to comfort her, gently saying, "Remember, my Eliza, you are a Christian."

God was on his mind. He asked a minister for Communion, and after an initial denial—the Church frowned on dueling—they granted his request. Angelica raced to the scene and stood vigil with Eliza, the Schuyler sisters together, with the man they both loved, for one last time. The seven surviving children were summoned, lining up in a row at the foot of the bed. He looked at them, choked with emotion, and then had to look away in pain.

A crowd gathered around the house on Jane Street, praying, mourning. The city grew quiet. In one of Hamilton's final lucid moments, he said, "I have no ill will against Colonel Burr . . . I met him with a fixed resolution to do him no harm. I forgive all that happened."

For hours he squirmed in pain. Eliza fanned his face, trying to cool the fever. Then came what might be the final words of Alexander Hamilton. The man who had worked most of his life to build the Union, to bond the states together, and to protect it from enemies, said that ". . . if they break this union, they will break my heart."

He died at 2 p.m., July 12, 1804. He was forty-seven years old.

Burr wasn't in the room. He had calmly returned to his home and sunk into his library, where he cracked open a book. He had a pleasant breakfast with his cousin. "Neither in his manner nor in his conversation was there any evidence of excitement or concern," the cousin later recalled. Hours later, the cousin passed through Wall Street, saw the grief-stricken crowd, and sensed that something awful had happened. A friend soon filled him in: "Colonel Burr has killed [Hamilton] in a duel this morning!" *Crazy talk*, the cousin thought—the two had just had breakfast, and Burr hadn't mentioned a word.

To get a better sense of the way Hamilton honored his country, as a contrast, it's worth tracing the later footsteps of Aaron Burr. He embarked on a curious journey. "I propose leaving town for a few days," he wrote to a friend, as if he needed a relaxing summer getaway. But he soon realized that the duel had driven him "into a sort of exile" that might cause a "permanent ostracism." So he quietly traveled to New Jersey, then Philadelphia, where he hunkered down anonymously. He traveled at night, in secret, and wore a dark cloak. A grand jury soon charged the vice president with "willful murder."

Burr, at this point, had two very clear options. He could surrender himself and plead his case, arguing—with some merit—that while dueling is technically illegal, it's also a time-honored custom that hardly counts as *murder*. Or he could go into hiding.

He did neither of these things. Instead, Burr hatched a plan to "seize the nearly 1 million square miles of the Louisiana Purchase . . . and to turn them into Aaron Burr's personal empire," explains Sedgwick. "The ambition was inspired by Napoléon, then overrunning Europe. Burr would call himself emperor as well, with Theodosia [his daughter] his empress, and her son, Aaron Burr Alston, the heir to the throne."

This was more than just daydreaming. Burr realized that while he had succeeded in killing Alexander Hamilton, he had killed his own career with the same bullet. So he needed new friends. He told a British agent that he would happily serve the Crown if they would help him "effect a Separation of the Western Part of the United States." He also had his eye on Florida. Burr, his reputation in tatters, would travel south and conquer the American frontier.

Incredibly, in the midst of all of this, while he was wanted for murder in New Jersey, Burr quietly made his way back to the new capital in Washington, D.C., and actually presided over the US Senate. He dined with Jefferson. (What, we wonder, would they clink glasses and celebrate?) While wanted for murder, he presided over the impeachment trial of a Supreme Court justice.

Once his term officially ended, Burr traveled south, met with coconspirators, and fleshed out a plan to attack Mexico. He bided his time. In 1806 he met a young senator named Andrew Jackson and tried to enlist him in the cause. (Jackson demurred.) Burr sent ciphered letters to generals. Then one of his conspirators betrayed him, revealing the evidence to President Jefferson. The jig was up. Jefferson ordered that Aaron Burr be arrested and tried for the crime of treason.

Again Burr went into hiding. One witness said he was "disguised in an old blanket coat begirt with a leathern strap, to which a tin cup was suspended on the left and a scalping knife on the right." He was caught in this very outfit.

Burr was officially tried for treason. The verdict? Not guilty. It boiled down to a lack of hard evidence; treason, as defined by Article III of the Constitution, had to be proven by "the testimony of two witnesses," and Chief Justice Marshall decided that Burr's treason "is not proved by a single witness." (Someone who would have likely approved of that verdict: Alexander Hamilton. The law is the law.)

Burr might have been exonerated on a legal technicality, but he was never again truly free. He was broke, hated, and taunted by angry mobs. He sailed across the Atlantic and took refuge in

Europe, ping-ponging from city to city. He dodged his creditors, he tried (in vain) to make political connections, and he seduced more women. He requested an audience with Napoléon—denied. He requested an audience with King George—denied. He was nearly sent to debtors' prison. He made a few bucks by translating English to French. At one point he lived on tea, bread, and a "single egg for dinner."

In 1812 he returned to America, where he hunkered down in relative obscurity. A contemporary found him to be "shriveled into the dimensions of a dwarf." He kept seducing women. In 1833, at the age of seventy-seven, he married once again—this time for money. She soon divorced him. The divorce must have been a blow, as it was his last thread to financial security. On the day of Burr's death, the divorce papers were finalized by a lawyer named . . . Alexander Hamilton Jr.

LEAVE A MARK

—

"We can never get rid of his financial system."

—THOMAS JEFFERSON

IN THE DAYS AND weeks after Hamilton's death, New York mourned its fallen leader.

"There was as much or more lamentation than as when George Washington died," one witness remembered. People wore black armbands. Merchants closed shop. (Less sorrowful was Thomas Jefferson, who barely commented on the event, casually writing to a friend of "remarkable deaths lately." John Adams wrote, "No one wished to get rid of Hamilton in *that* way.")

On the water, British and French gunships fired their cannons in salute. A large crowd filed into Trinity Church, where Hamilton remains buried today, for the somber funeral. Gouverneur Morris gave the eulogy; this was the man who, many years before, had tapped Washington on the shoulder on Hamilton's mischievous dare.

Morris asked the crowd a question that, in some ways, channeled the idea for this very book: He asked the citizens to think about their own lives, and whenever they had a decision to make, they should ask themselves, "Would Hamilton have done this thing?" (WWHD?) His eulogy summed up Hamilton's grand themes: "Knowing the purity of his heart, he bore it, as it were, in his hand, exposing to every passenger its inmost recesses."

That nails it. The *purity of his heart* was exposed to every passenger. For better and worse, Hamilton wore his heart on his (beautifully cuffed) sleeve, confident in his beliefs, daring any to challenge him.

Remember all the fighting over banks? Once he settled into the White House, President Jefferson dispatched his brilliant new treasury secretary, Albert Gallatin, to finally, at long last, root out the corruption of Hamilton's financial system. He ordered him to dig through the records and find "the blunders and frauds of Hamilton." Now Jefferson would have his revenge.

Gallatin was loyal to Jefferson. So he pored through the files. He read through all the archives and doubled-checked and triple-checked. Finally he gave his report to President Jefferson.

"Well, Gallatin, what have you found?" the President asked.

We can imagine Gallatin clearing his throat. "I have found the most perfect system ever formed," he began. "Any change that should be made in it would injure it. Hamilton made no blunders, committed no frauds. He did nothing wrong." (As Gallatin later recalled, "I think Mr. Jefferson was disappointed.")

Even beyond the grave, Hamilton left a mark, and he left it with honor. Jefferson tried to erase that mark, but he couldn't. "We can never get rid of his financial system," he groaned, defeated. Jefferson would pay his rival an eternal backhanded compliment, installing a bust of Hamilton at Monticello, directly across from a bust of himself, so the two Founders would stare each other down, eye to eye, until the end of time.

"In later U.S. history, there were attempts to get rid of elements of Hamilton's financial system. They always came back," explains financial historian Richard Sylla. "Today, public credit, the dollar, the banking system, the central bank, the securities markets, and the corporate system, although none of them is without problems, remain the envy of the world."

Hamilton's mark goes far beyond the world of finance. Without *The Federalist Papers* and Hamilton's inspired defense, we might not have a ratified Constitution. Without Hamilton, we might not have a federal government strong enough to preserve the Union. "He was one of the greatest American constitutional lawyers—not surprisingly, since he helped write the Constitution," writes Brookhiser. "If John Marshall was the father of judicial review, Hamilton was the grandfather . . . He deserves a statue in front of the Supreme Court almost as much as his statue at the Treasury Department."

America needed *both* Jefferson's idealism and Hamilton's realism. "Jefferson was the poet of the American founding; Hamilton was the nation builder who infused the essential elements of permanence and stability into the American system," concludes historian Stephen F. Knott. "Alexander Hamilton made the twentieth century the American century."

Even more remarkable than his accomplishments, however, is the *way* he brought them about. His life inspires. From the time he was a clerk to the day he took a bullet, Hamilton's maxims rarely wavered: Seek the core principles, turn grit into genius, hide nothing, move quick, say what you believe (no matter the cost), value what's right over what's popular, and close with a flourish.

Not every single one of Hamilton's maxims, of course, explicitly translates to our daily lives. (Please don't instruct your child to fight in a duel.) Yet the broad contours are clear.

"Sometimes I wake up at 6:30 in the morning and I don't want to get up, and I'm lying in my bed," says Douglas Hamilton. "Then I'll think of that letter that Alexander Hamilton wrote to his son—about how to schedule your day, starting at 6 a.m. And I get up."

Hamilton was a genius. Yet that's not what made him great. He worked harder to give himself an edge, he viewed the world through a wider lens, he read more books, and then he got back to work. All of us can do this. Remember Plutarch: "The virtues of these great men serve me as a sort of looking glass, in which I may see how to adjust and adorn my own life."

Even when it comes to the duel, we can glean some wisdom. The point is not that you should grab a pistol or use a *delope*. The point is that you should believe in something—whatever it is—with so much passion, so much love, so much hunger, that you would be willing to die for it. Hamilton believed in the United States of America. He believed in his family. He believed in steady improvement *if the projector is constant*. What do you believe in? Is the projector constant?

CODA

—

FOR OVER TWO HUNDRED years, Alexander Hamilton has been the most underrated Founding Father. Now, of course, there are some who wonder if he has suddenly become *overrated*. Is he overexposed?

Nope. Not even close. After writing this book, I'm convinced that Alexander Hamilton is one of the main reasons—maybe *the* reason—that we are the United States, not just some united states. He's the reason that we do more in America than just plant cabbage and herd sheep. With astonishing foresight that eclipsed every other Founding Father's—Washington, Adams, Jefferson, all of them—Hamilton envisioned the future of the United States. Then he made it happen.

As part of my research, I traveled to the islands of Nevis and St. Croix, in the West Indies, for a pilgrimage to the birthplace of Alexander Hamilton. I traced his footsteps and visited where he grew up, where he went to the doctor's, where his mother was imprisoned, where he had his first job at the trading shop of Beekman and Cruger, where he weighed the ships' cargo, and where he set sail for America. I wanted to breathe the air he breathed. I hoped that this would give me a better understanding of the essence of the man.

It did and it didn't.

Yes, it's true that on Nevis, next to his childhood home, I could sit on the rocks and gaze at the clear blue sea, and this view, more or less, would be what Alex could see as a boy. Perhaps he stared across the water and dreamed of a larger world. I closed my eyes and tried to feel him in my bones . . . and it felt a little forced.

Then I flew back to New York, deplaned at JFK, and took a cab to Brooklyn. The skyline felt like an old friend. One World Trade Center. The Empire State Building. The Brooklyn Bridge. They all seemed to welcome me home, and suddenly I felt chills. *This* is Alexander Hamilton. This is the world he envisioned. While his rivals pined for a land of goats and cotton (and slaves), Hamilton had prophesied this land of commerce, industry, progress, and opportunity. I didn't need to travel to Nevis or St. Croix. He has been here all along. The nation has his soul. I'm not the first to say it and I hope I won't be the last: We are now living in Alexander Hamilton's America.

ACKNOWLEDGMENTS

THERE ARE THREE MEN who deserve a special category of thanks; if they had not been born, this book would not exist. The first is Alexander Hamilton. The second is Ron Chernow. The third is Lin-Manuel Miranda. Hamilton gave us modern America, Chernow's book introduced me to Hamilton, and Miranda, well, you know the fruits of his genius. Thank you, sirs.

One of Hamilton's favorite words was "Herculean." So I want to give a *Herculean* thanks to my incredible agent, Rob Weisbach, for believing in this idea, and me, from Day One. Rob, you made this a better book and me a better writer. Thank you. And I'm in a massive debt—(debt: "a national blessing") to my amazing editor, Matt Inman, who worked tirelessly to whip this book into shape. Matt, you always saw the big picture while relentlessly attacking the details—very Hamiltonian.

Thanks to everyone else on the all-star team at Three Rivers Press, including marketing pros Julie Cepler and Seanie Civale, editorial life-saver Julia Elliott, publicity rock stars Tammy Blake and Rebecca Marsh, production supervisor Kevin Garcia, cover designer Jake Nicolella (love it, Jake), interior designer Andrea Lau, art director Elizabeth Rendfleisch, production editor Mark McCauslin, and to everyone else behind the scenes for all their hard work. You all honored two of Hamilton's maxims: *Move quick* and *Command the details*. Thank you.

Special thanks to the Alexander Hamilton Awareness Society, including founder Rand Scholet and vice president Nicole Scholet de Villavicencio. I learned so much from you. Thank you for sharing your encyclopedic knowledge, your researching tips and tricks, and your infectious joy of our forgotten Founding Father. Thanks to Bob White, president of the Alexander Hamilton Society of St. Croix, for giving me a world-class tour of Hamilton's teenage stomping grounds, and thanks to Evelyn Henville, executive director of the Nevis Historical and Conservation Society, for introducing me to his birthplace.

Thanks to historian Michael E. Newton for your dogged research and helpful advice, to financial historian Richard Sylla for your elucidating thoughts on Hamilton's financing system, and a great-great-great-great-great deal of thanks to Hamilton's great-great-great-great-great-grandson, Douglas Hamilton. Thank you, sir, for sharing thoughts on your ancestor. No "guidebook" could ever truly do your ancestor justice, but I hope this tacks in the right direction.

I gobbled up many Hamilton books and materials, but a special shout-out to the works of Richard Brookhiser, Michael E. Newton, Joanne B. Freeman, Stephen F. Knott, John Sedgwick, Thomas Fleming, and of course Ron Chernow.

Thanks to the good friends who were generous (or foolish?) enough to read early drafts of the manuscript and provide valuable feedback. You sharpened it, challenged it, polished it. More Herculean thanks to: Rand Scholet (I can't thank you enough for the careful vetting, thoughts, and measured feedback), Nicole Scholet de Villavicencio (ditto), Keith Meatto ("How many years? . . ."), Joe Hall (sorry I couldn't include the ". . . holster" line), Catherine Perez (we're overdue for some Kingfishers), Lisa Schiller (I owe you whiskey), Josh Wilbur (a productive train ride; thank you), Laura Strausfeld (your energy gave me energy), Terry Selucky (meant a lot to me), Michael Curran (while in a courtroom!), Braxton Robbason (while injured!), Rochelle Bilow (our streak lives), Jen Doll (while on the beach!), Kate Mays (while starting a new job!), Isabelle Puckett (here's to red-eye flights . . .), Preeti Chhibber (sorry there aren't more puns), Laura Demoreuille (obvs), Joy Parisi (I will take your compliment to the grave),

Cody Dolan (ace comments, as always), and Dolly Chugh (your enthusiasm throughout has truly inspired me). Thank you, all of you.

I researched and wrote this book in a frenzied burst of time, and that could not have happened without the support of my family and friends. Eternal thanks to my parents, stepparents, sisters and brother, cousins, aunts and uncles. Thanks to Shawn Regruto and the Wednesday Night Writer's Group. To the Paragraph writer's space. To the lifelong Texas/FFL gang of Eric Pedersen (Hamilton: "the first duty of society is justice"), Chris Shaver, Todd Rinaldo, Dan Abbruscato, Walker Robinson, James Mangano, Trevor Hoff (I know you're not a Texan, but work with me here), Tania Hoff, Charlie Applegate, Joe Hall, and Cody Dolan.

To Jamie Davis and Evan Aronowitz; to Keith Meatto, Curtis Sparrer, Leo Lopez, Paul Jarrett, Lee Bob Black; to Adam Smith, Matt Smith, Kabir Merchant, Erik Brown, Teddy Vuong, Omer Mohammed, Dave Spinks, Stephane Conte, and Wes Hollomon. To my old coauthor and constant source of inspiration Andrea Syrtash, to Amy Braunschweiger, Brian Sack, Stephanie Meyers (I still owe you for the original *MF* nudge), Elizabeth Meggs (constant good vibes), Laura Brounstein, Jo, Meghan Miller, Toni (for listening to me drone on), and to Allison Joy, for letting me take an editorial leave of absence, of sorts, from *Comstock's*. (Thanks to Christine for the well-timed gift; it did indeed inspire.)

A big thanks, of course, for putting up with all my Hamilton talk at the proverbial water cooler: thanks to Michael Sang, Betsy Poris, Juliet Nuss, Harry McNeil, Traci Swain, Shandy Qu, Ann-Marie Resnick, Ellie Chamberland, Wayne Friedman, Mike White, and the rest of the mighty crew at Scholastic.

Once last thanks: to Eliza Hamilton. If she had not fought for her husband's legacy, none of this would exist.

To all of you, I Remain your Obedient Servant,

Jeff Wilser

NOTES

—

It SHOULD BE CLEAR by now, I hope, that this is not an academic or scholarly work. Thanks to the tireless, dogged work of historians like Ron Chernow, Michael E. Newton, James Flexner, Richard Brookhiser, and Stephen Knott, the arc of Hamilton's life is now less of a mystery. I am in awe of the actual, proper biographers—the brave men and women who spend years triple-checking primary sources, cross-checking letters against public records, looking at dusty old parchments, and squinting at microfiche. (Confession: I'm not totally sure how to work a microfiche machine.)

My role is to synthesize, curate, add perspective, and hopefully add a touch of levity. So for much of the Hamilton journey, I cobbled together the basics from Chernow, Flexner, Newton, Brookhiser, Knott, Broadus Mitchell, Forrest McDonald, Thomas Fleming (especially helpful for the duel), and Hamilton's son (John C. Hamilton) and grandson (Allan McLane Hamilton). I supplemented all of this, of course, by studying Hamilton's letters and manifestos. Joanne Freeman edited a crisp edition of the essential papers (*Alexander Hamilton: Writings;* it clocks in at only 1,108 pages, and for Hamilton that's short), and I read many obscure, mundane letters (that sometimes contain hidden gems) via the amazing resource at Founders.Archives.gov. (Thank you, Rand Scholet, for showing me this wonderful tool. It really is life-changing.)

The below notes, then, are intended to add the occasional bits of clarification, cite the key quotes, and explain some nuances that I summarized in the main text. Hamilton, no doubt, would read these endnotes, curl his lip, and say, "Worthless. Drunkard." But I hope you find them useful.

Note on spelling and capitalizations:

The spellings of many old letters are funky. That's the result of either: (1) archaic spellings that were correct back then; or (2) simple mistakes, as the letters were, at times, written in haste, and the parchment didn't come with spell-check. The Founders also tend to Capitalize random Words in the middle of the Sentences. As both of these tics are distracting, I've generally Cleaned things up unless the originals are too charming not to Inxlude.

INTRODUCTION

xiii Obama quote—the *New York Times*, November 19, 2015. Full quote is worth reading: "[The Hamilton musical] is brilliant, and so much so that I'm pretty sure this is the only thing that Dick Cheney and I have agreed on—during my entire political career—it speaks to this vibrancy of American democracy, but also the fact that it was made by these living, breathing, flawed individuals who were brilliant. We haven't seen a collection of that much smarts and chutzpah and character in any other nation in history, I think."

xiv "Taught himself Latin"—perhaps he also used tutors and the prep school to learn Latin, but this refers to his mad-dash studies to get into college, compensating for a lack of formal education in the West Indies.

xv The word "maxim" appears 209 times in *The Complete Works of Alexander Hamilton*—counted via Kindle search.

xv " 'Tis my maxim to let the naked truth . . ."—from "A Full Vindication," December 15, 1774, *Papers of Alexander Hamilton* (*PAH*).

xv "It is a maxim of my life to enjoy the present good . . ."—letter to Eliza, July 6, 1780, *PAH*.

xv ". . . maxim, that there is three to one in favor . . ."—letter to Gouverneur Morris, September 1, 1777.

xv Richard Brookhiser deserves tremendous credit for first making the Plutarch/Hamilton connection; his commentary here (and elsewhere) is from his biography, *Alexander Hamilton, American*.

xvi Quotes from Douglas Hamilton via personal interview (May 24, 2016).

xvii I've been lucky enough to have multiple conversations and exchanges with Rand Scholet—the most energetic and enthusiastic Hamiltonian on the planet. Do check out the Alexander Hamilton Awareness Society and its website, AllThingsHamilton.com.

1. SELF-IMPROVEMENT

RISE ABOVE YOUR STATION

3 Quote—letter to Edward Stevens, November 11, 1769, *PAH*.

3 Historians have traditionally spelled Hamilton's mother's name as Rachel Faucette, but more recently, Michael E. Newton's research suggests Rachael Fawcett.

3 "Whoring with everyone" is from Lavien's divorce papers, via Flexner.

3 There's some debate about whether Rachael was accused of adultery *before* she was thrown in jail, or only after she lived with James Hamilton. It's possible she was thrown into prison not for adultery, but for failing to be a proper wife. (Either way, the first husband, John Lavien, sounds like a real keeper!)

3 "This wasn't a happy home" refers to the inferred cruelty of John Lavien (Rachael's first husband). There's no evidence (that I've seen) suggesting Rachael herself was cruel or a bad mother. To the contrary, we can imagine her as a woman of strength, intelligence (inferred from her library), and independence, who had to overcome the sexist norms of the eighteenth century.

4 Quote from Flexner—here and elsewhere—via *The Young Hamilton—A Biography*.

4 "Alcohol for her head" courtesy of Newton.

6 Doug Hamilton quotes—personal interview.

STEAL (NEW SKILLS) FROM EVERY JOB

7 Quote—as reported by his son John C. Hamilton in Hamilton's first biography.

7 The basics are again pulled from the big guns of Flexner, Chernow, Newton, Brookhiser—supplemented by a phone interview with Michael Newton.

8 I've been inside the Scale House. I *think* the scale inside is the original that Hamilton used, but I'm not confident so didn't mention that in the text.

8   "Frisbee toss away" is my own estimate. (It would indeed be a long Frisbee toss, but it could be done.)

8   "Worse parcel of mules . . ."—letter to Nicholas Cruger, 1772, *PAH*.

8   On the "watch your slaves pick cotton" commentary . . . It's true that young Hamilton's work, too, involved slaves. Discussed later in the Embrace Equality section.

SIDEBAR: WHEN WAS HAMILTON BORN?

10   The debate over the age is mostly outside the scope of this book, so I quickly summarized so we can move on to the good stuff.

10   Newton's *Alexander Hamilton: The Formative Years* has a far more nuanced analysis with a meticulous breakdown of all the facts. (He also comes down on the side of 1757.)

10   My own humble editorializing: Hamilton, like all of us, had many flaws. Yet he's not really a "liar"; in fact, he tells the truth even when it hurts him. (Exhibit A: the Reynolds pamphlet; Exhibit B: Aaron Burr.) Lying about his age to appear more like a child prodigy seems at odds with nearly everything else we know about the man.

READ WHEN OTHERS PLAY

11   Quote—letter to Eliza, July 2–4, 1780, *PAH*.

11   The contents of the thirty-four-book library suggested by Chernow.

12   Quotes from Chernow—here and elsewhere—via *Alexander Hamilton*.

12   Reading math—it's true that the average page might have more than 250 words, depending upon the book's format. These estimates are ballpark.

UNLEASH YOUR HOBBIES

16   Quote—letter to William Hamilton, May 2, 1797, *PAH*.

17   "Artful little slut" poem—from Hamilton (or, technically, "A.H.") to the *Royal Danish American Gazette*, April 6, 1771.

18   Hurricane letter—from Alexander Hamilton to the *Royal Danish American Gazette*, September 6, 1772.

18   The traditional tale of the hurricane is wonderfully told in Chernow; more recently, Newton has meticulously stitched together a timeline suggesting that the hurricane, in fact, happened *after*

the funds had already been raised for Hamilton's scholarship. If that's the case, it's even more a testament to the power of Hamilton's hard work at the trading shop.

TURN GRIT INTO GENIUS

20 Quote—from Oral History, *Manual of Useful Information* (1893), via William Chrystal's Alexander Hamilton's Rules for Living, http://william-g-chrystal.com/uploads/3/1/0/2/3102605/alexander_hamiltons_rules_for_living.pdf; also *The Pennsylvania Gazette* (Volume 15, Issue 12, 1917). It's possible that this quote is a paraphrase, as it has been tough to track down in primary sources.

20 John Adams quote from *The Adams Papers, Diary and Autobiography of John Adams, vol. 2, 1771–1781,* ed. L. H. Butterfield. Cambridge: Harvard University Press, 1961, pp. 108–109.

22 The "I have often heard him speak of . . . anatomy" quote from Dr. Hosack, the same family physician who would go with him to Weehawken for the duel.

SIDEBAR: THE RULES FOR MR. PHILIP HAMILTON, AGE 18

23 Amazing schedule, right?

23 Rules for Philip Hamilton, 1800, *PAH.*

DRINK UP THE FACTS

24 Quote—from "Pay Book of the State Company of Artillery," 1777, *PAH.*

24 The bulk of the quotes are from the army pay book.

25 "must have been a blockhead" from Allan McLane Hamilton's biography; the full quote is "A man must have been a blockhead who would part with such a valuable lien knowingly."

26 Princeton study and Michael Friedman quote via the *Wall Street Journal,* "Can Handwriting Make You Smarter?" April 4, 2016, by Robert Lee Hotz.

DON'T JOIN THE CLUB, MAKE THE CLUB

27 Quote—letter to George Clinton, May 14, 1783.

27 Flexner provides the context and the quote from Troup.

28 John C. Hamilton biography provides the story of the speech in The Fields.

SEEK THE CORE PRINCIPLES

30   Quote—this baby comes straight from "The Farmer Refuted," *PAH.*

31   Rest of the content is from "The Farmer Refuted" and "A Full Vindication."

30   "very pompous"—Chernow's description.

32   Quote from Newton—here and elsewhere—via *Alexander Hamilton: The Formative Years.*

33   "Became our oracle" quote is from Sons of Liberty big shot Marinus Willett, first cited by John C. Hamilton.

CHAPTER 2—CAREER ADVANCEMENT

MOVE QUICK

37   Full quote: "I hate procrastination in business & wish it to be terminated either by the completion or dissolution of the Bargain."—letter to Joseph Anthony, March 11,1795, *PAH.*

37   Flexner provides a detailed picture of the skirmish with the *Asia.*

38   The $8 beer at Fraunces Tavern, alas, is from my own bar tab.

39   The Venn diagram analysis is my own summation.

SAY WHAT YOU BELIEVE, NO MATTER THE COST

40   Quote—from "A Full Vindication," *PAH.*

42   "Men are fond of going with the stream"—letter to James Wilson, January 25, 1789, *PAH.*

SEE THE FOREST AND THE TREES

43   Quote—also from "A Full Vindication," *PAH.*

43   "most beautiful model of discipline"—from Robert Troup.

44   "I noticed a youth, a mere stripling . . ."—originally from Washington Irving's biography of George Washington.

44   "Circumstances of our country" prediction—from "The Farmer Refuted," actually one year *before* the fighting even started.

FIND A WORTHY MENTOR

47   Quote—letter to James Duane, October 1, 1779, *PAH.*

48   "Frank, affable, intelligent"—Senator Harrison Gray Otis, via Chernow.

48   Burr despising Washington—letter from John Adams to Benjamin Rush, August 23, 1805.

49   "Hamilton had to *think* as well as to *write* for him . . ."—Adjutant General Timothy Pickering.

SIDEBAR: "HAMILTON. ALEXANDER HAMILTON."

50   The basics come from Newton, Chernow, Flexner; Newton deserves credit for the amazing CIA quote.

PICK UP THE SLACK

51   Quote—reported in Newton, Chernow, Flexner.

51   The diary of the Valley Forge soldier comes from Flexner.

52   "I hold it an established maxim . . . in favor of the party attacking"—letter to Gouverneur Morris, September 1, 1777, *PAH*.

53   Clarification: During Lee's initial attack, Washington and Hamilton waited at the headquarters of the larger body of the American army.

53   "By God, they are flying from a shadow!" via Newton; "damned poltroon" dialogue via Chernow.

54   "never saw the General to so much advantage . . ."—letter to Elias Boudinot, July 5, 1778.

SIDEBAR: HAMILTON'S FIRST DUEL

56   "earwigs" and "toad eaters" via Brookhiser.

56   The 20 percent fatality study comes via Thomas Fleming.

56   "ten paces" is an assumption from the traditional paces required by duel etiquette—courtesy Joanne Freeman.

56   The "Upon the whole, dueling is great!" quote (paraphrase) is technically a joint statement published by Hamilton and John Laurens's second, Evan Edwards, on December 24, 1778.

EXIT WITH CLASS

57   Quote—letter to James McHenry, February 18, 1781, *PAH*.

58   The key description of the quarrel on the staircase—letter to Philip Schuyler, February 18, 1781, *PAH*.

GO TO WAR FOR YOUR PROMOTION

60   Quote—letter to John Jay, August 27, 1798.

60   "It has become necessary to me to apply . . ."—letter to Washington, April 27, 1781, *PAH*.

62   British soldier quote ("legs had been shot off") via Chernow.

63   "made such a terrible yell" quote via Flexner.

3. ROMANCE

SEDUCE WITH YOUR STRENGTHS

66 Quote—the amazing "ALL FOR LOVE" (actually in caps) is from a letter to Catharine (Kitty) Livingston, May 1777, *PAH*. Ditto for the other romantic passages.

67 "A rainy evening" quote from Flexner.

67 "love-making was evidently pursued with the same activity . . ." from grandson (and biographer) Allan McLane Hamilton.

68 John Adams "debauched morals" quote—a letter to Abigail Adams, January 9, 1797.

68 The epic "whores enough to draw off" Adams quote—letter to Benjamin Rush, November 11, 1806.

KNOW WHAT YOU WANT, GET WHAT YOU NEED

69 Every gem in this entry is from one glorious letter: Hamilton to John Laurens, April 1779, *PAH*.

71 Editors at the National Archive suggest that the "I must not publish the whole of this" note was "presumably written by John C. Hamilton," but technically it's not definitive.

LOVE WITHOUT LABELS

72 Quote—"action rather than words to convince you that I love you," as well as the following bromantic passages, in the same letter to Laurens, April 1779.

72 Laurens's Geneva curriculum quote ("experimental philosophy")—Flexner.

74 "friendly intercourse with your honorable body"—address from Washington to the Massachusetts General Court, April 1, 1776.

74 Washington quote about Lafayette—from George Washington to Marie-Joseph-Paul-Yves-Roch-Gilbert du Motier, marquis de Lafayette, January 4, 1782.

74 The amazing "kissed him from ear to ear" quote is from St. George Tucker, courtesy of the indomitable Michael E. Newton.

75 "dances with, and kisses (*filthy* beast!) those of his own sex"—via Brookhiser.

SIDEBAR: THE LADIES OF AARON BURR

76 John Sedgwick paints a vivid (and unsettling) portrait of Burr's love life in *War of Two: Alexander Hamilton, Aaron Burr, and the Duel That Stunned the Nation*. This section is in his debt.

FLATTER YOUR WAY TO HER HEART

78   Quote—letter to Elizabeth Schuyler, March 17, 1780, *PAH.*
78   Also—letter to Eliza, July 2–4, 1780, *PAH.*
78   Also—letter to Eliza, September 6, 1781, *PAH.*
78   "lively dark eyes"—from Tench Tilghman, via Chernow.
80   Philip Schuyler's quote via Chernow.

FLIRT WITH THE LINE . . . BUT NEVER CROSS IT

81   Quote—letter to Angelica Church, October 2, 1791, *PAH.*
81   "Nose of the Grecian mold" quote—via Brookhiser.
82   Angelica's "lend him to me for a little while"—via Allan McLane Hamilton, ditto for the "sprightly correspondence" quotes.
83   "last theme of our conversation"—letter to Angelica Church, November 8, 1789.
83   "my beautiful brunettes," via Sedgwick.

4. MONEY

CONVICTIONS FIRST. CASH SECOND

87   Quote—via Reminiscences of James A. Hamilton
88   "one twelfth the number of prostitutes" gem—Brookhiser.
90   "soared far above all competition"—then-clerk and eventual judge James Kent.

BEWARE SPECULATION

91   Quote—letter to William Seton, August 16, 1791, *PAH.*
92   Report from his son, John C. Hamilton.
92   As Chernow marvels in amazement: "That Alexander Hamilton opted to purchase land in the far northern woods and bungled the chance to buy dirt-cheap Manhattan real estate must certainly count as one of his few conspicuous failures of economic judgment."

FIND TIME FOR THE QUILLS AND THE BILLS

93   Quote—from *The Federalist Papers,* No. 15.
94   The precise breakdown of *The Federalists Papers'* authorship is still disputed by scholars; this estimate is from Chernow. (Ditto for Eliza's letter about him writing on the boat.)

SIDEBAR: HAMILTON THE MONARCHIST?

96   Basics here from Chernow, Brookhiser, McDonald.

CONQUER THE CREDIT

97 Quote—letter to Robert Morris, April 30, 1781, *PAH*.

99 Note—technically Hamilton did not personally read the "Report on Credit" to Congress, as there was a concern of blurring Legislative and Executive lines.

99 "administrative genius" quote—biographer Jacob E. Cooke.

100 Jefferson quote—from "Notes on the State of Viriginia."

100 Adams anti-banking—letter to Benjamin Rush, August 28, 1811.

WHAT'S FREE TODAY WILL COST YOU TOMORROW

102 Quote—letter to Henry Lee, December 1, 1789.

GIVE WITHOUT FANFARE

104 Quote—letter to Samuel Hodgdon, February 22, 1783, *PAH* (first shown to me by Nicole Scholet de Villavicencio).

104 Ralph Earl story from James Hamilton.

105 *New York Times* piece—"What 'Hamilton' Forgets About Hamilton," by Jason Frank and Isaac Kramnick, June 10, 2016.

105 Aaron Burr kicker from John C. Hamilton.

DON'T SKIMP ON THE LIFE INSURANCE

106 Quote—letter to Angelica Church, March 6, 1795, *PAH*.

107 "allot myself" quote—same letter to Angelica.

107 Quote about Eliza's financial skills—letter from James McHenry to Hamilton, January 3, 1791 (hat tip to Nicole Scholet de Villavicencio).

107 Chernow provides the Eliza aftermath and the secret that was kept until 1937.

108 Jefferson Pilot Insurance acquiring Hamilton Life Insurance—via Bloomberg, http://www.bloomberg.com/research/stocks/private/snapshot.asp?privcapId=35383169.

OWN THE DEBT, DON'T LET THE DEBT OWN YOU

109 Quote—letter to Robert Morris, April 30, 1781, *PAH*.

109 The basics here are well covered elsewhere, supplemented by my interview with financial historian Richard Sylla.

CHAPTER 5: STYLE & ETIQUETTE

LOOK THE PART, ACT THE PART

115 Quote—letter to James McHenry, May 18, 1799, *PAH.*

115 "dressed in a blue coat with bright buttons"—from Henry Jones Ford.

116 The delightful uniform descriptions—from "Enclosure: Uniform of the Army of the United States, December 1799," *PAH.*

CARRY YOURSELF WITH DIGNITY, NOT DISGUST

118 Quote—letter to Washington, May 5, 1789, *PAH.* Ditto for all the rules.

120 "Drumstick" quote is from the diary of Senator William Maclay, first via Allan McLane Hamilton.

SPRINKLE IN THE CHARM

122 Quote—letter to Eliza, October 2, 1780.

122 "Voice exceedingly pleasant" is from James Parton's nineteenth-century biography of Aaron Burr, via Sedgwick.

123 Judge Kent anecdote has been widely shared; I first saw it in Chernow.

123 Rest of the "charming" quotes from Hammie's letters to Eliza.

SEAL THE DEAL OVER DINNER

124 Quote—letter to Colonel Hugh Hughes (what a great name), November 1781, *PAH.*

124 Joanne Freeman quote—here and elsewhere—via *Affairs of Honor: National Politics in the New Republic.*

124 Letter to senator—letter to Robert Morris, November 9, 1790, *PAH.*

124 Adams's amazing "young girl . . . trinkets" insults—letter to Benjamin Rush, January 25, 1806.

125 "Gladiators" again from the diary of Senator Maclay.

127 The push for the name "Hamiltoniana" was more in the afterglow of the Constitution ratification, not the Grand Dinner Bargain, but the point remains: Hamilton was at the peak of his powers.

GROOM WITH GUSTO

128 Quote—letter to James McHenry, August 13, 1799, *PAH*.

128 "John Wood shaved and dressed me . . ."—"The bearer John Wood" letter to Tobias Lear, October 29, 1790, *PAH*.

CLOSE WITH A FLOURISH

130 Quote—as reported in nineteenth-century biography from Henry Cabot Lodge.

RELISH THE ARTS

133 Quote—letter to John Laurens (describing the dignity of Major André, the British spy who would be executed), October 11, 1780, *PAH*.

133 Grandson quote—Allan McLane Hamilton.

133 "Art galleries," of course, wouldn't quite be what they are today, and likely just meant that they visited the home or shop of an artist. But still.

134 Angelica quote and "merry month of May" vignette via Chernow.

SIDEBAR: THE ORIGINAL DREAM TEAM

135 The "starting lineup" is my own editorializing and of course can be debated.

135 As Rand Scholet contends, "Adams' eight years as VP were void of accomplishment . . . and John Jay was the fourth most important founder in creating the US we live in today; hate to give him bench status." Who wants to join me in a "Fantasy Founding Fathers" league?

MAKE TIME FOR MISCHIEF

136 Quote—letter to Oliver Wolcott, October 3, 1795. (Clarification: the word "mischief" almost always has a negative connotation in the Revolutionary era.)

136 "Natural coldness" is from Count William de Deux-Ponts, courtesy of Newton.

PARLEZ FRANÇAIS

138 Quote—letter to his daughter Angelica, November 1793, *PAH*.

138 Hamilton is not the only (or even primary) reason that Lafayette aided the American cause, of course, and Lafayette named his son after Washington.

BE COURTEOUS, SIR

140 Quote—take your pick; he signed letters like that all the time.

141 Letter from Burr to Hamilton, June 22, 1804.

6. LEISURE

143 If we want to get technical . . . of course Alexander Hamilton had plenty to say about leisure. (We know that he enjoyed wine with friends, that he read deeply, that he relaxed with his family.) This sweeping overgeneralization, though, does seem to fit the spirit of our favorite workaholic from St. Croix.

7. FRIENDS & FAMILY

PUT THE FATHER IN FOUNDING FATHER

149 Quote—letter to Eliza, October 25, 1801, *PAH*.

149 Description of baby Philip—letter to Richard Meade, August 27, 1782, *PAH*.

150 The lovely breakfast scene: from the writings of James A. Hamilton.

POUR A SECOND GLASS

152 Quote—letter to Nicholas Fish, March 1782, *PAH*.

153 Maxim to "enjoy the present good . . ."—letter to Eliza, July 6, 1780, *PAH*.

153 Not wanting to get drunk with the British—letter to Eliza, March 17, 1780, *PAH*.

FRIENDS BEFORE POLITICS

154 Quote—letter to Lafayette, April 28, 1798.

154 Newton has an excellent analysis of Hamilton's parentage in *The Formative Years*.

155 Letter from Angelica—via Allan McLane Hamilton.

156 "It is a hard thing for me to be separated . . ." and "embrace you again . . ."—Lafayette to Hamilton, May 24, 1788.

156 Jefferson quotes via Chernow.

157 "brotherly union to the last moment of my life"—Lafayette to "Hammie," August 12, 1798.

KISS FREELY

158 All of these plucked from the *PAH*. (And there are gobs more.)

SIDEBAR: ADDITIONAL HAMILTONIAN AWESOMENESS

160 Hamilton's arguments about truth-as-defense, of course, culminated in a courtroom battle that effectively pitted him against then-President Jefferson—just one of the many, many great stories that couldn't quite fit in a slim volume.

160 Haiti—The Schiller Institute, http://www.schillerinstitute.org/educ/hist/toussaint.html.

KNOW THE BEST MEDICINE

162 Quote—letter to Eliza (date uncertain; 1783–1789), *PAH*.

162 Life expectancy—James M. Volo and Dorothy Denneen Volo, *Family Life in 17th- and 18th-Century America,* Greenwood, 2005, p. 39.

162 Jefferson's mocking of Hamilton via John Ferling.

163 Doctor story via Chernow.

NEVER CHEAT

165 Quote—from the Reynolds pamphlet, 1797, *PAH*. Most quotes in this section, in fact, are from the infamous Reynolds papers.

8. LEADERSHIP

EMBRACE EQUALITY

173 Quote—*The Federalist Papers* no. 36, 1788. Technically Hamilton was not talking about race relations here, but the spirit of the quote feels consistent with his broader views.

173 20 percent of NYC in slavery—"1 in 5" households in Chernow, official NYC historical marker, etc.

174 "Not a man living . . ."—Washington letter to Robert Morris, April 12, 1786.

174 Hamilton living a hundred yards from slave market—my own ballpark estimate from traveling to his (believed) home in Nevis. I might have miscounted and it could be closer to two hundred yards. The point stands.

175 "Things *odious* or *immoral* are not to be presumed . . ."—"The Defence" No. III, July 29, 1795, *PAH*.

176 Jefferson's unsettling quotes about the races—from "Notes on the State of Virginia," www.pbs.org/wgbh/aia/part3/3h490t.html.

FIND THE IMPLIED POWER

178 Quote—"Final Version of an Opinion on the Constitutionality of an Act to Establish a Bank," February 23, 1791, *PAH.*

178 Bankers should "suffer death accordingly"—letter from Jefferson to James Madison, October 1, 1792.

SIDEBAR: MEANWHILE, AT AARON BURR'S HOUSE . . .

181 Burr lacking "many (or any) signature issues" is of course subjective, and overlooks his (relatively) progressive attitude toward women's rights. Compared to Hamilton and the other Founding Fathers, though, he was generally silent.

BEING RIGHT TRUMPS BEING POPULAR

182 Quote—letter to Washington, November 11, 1794, *PAH.*

COMMAND THE DETAILS

186 Quote—"Enclosure II: [Statement Showing the Particular Periods when the Bonds Were Distributed]," January 3, 1792, *PAH.*

186 All the mint goodies from "Report on the Establishment of a Mint," January 28, 1791, *PAH.*

188 Coast Guard details—Treasury Department Circular to the Collectors of the Customs, June 1, 1791, *PAH.*

189 The eagle-eyed Chernow pointed out the Cuban Missile Crisis connection.

189 "Hamilton's Charge" was first pointed out to me by Nicole Scholet de Villavicencio; also on official Coast Guard documents like http://www.uscgnews.com/external/content/document/4007/1444219/1/CG_Great%20LakesBoardingsFinal.pdf.

BARKIN' BEATS BITIN'

190 Quote—letter to James McHenry, March 18, 1799, *PAH.*

190 Checklist is my own humble exhibit, and certainly oversimplifies.

191 Technically the "Dolls, dressed and undressed" list was not from the original announcement of the whiskey tax, but the "Report Relative to the Additional Supplies for the Ensuing Year, 16 March 1792." *PAH.* Same vibe.

194 "Barkin' beats bitin'"—as told to me while walking through Hamilton's old childhood streets, by the amazing Bob White, head of the St. Croix chapter of the Alexander Hamilton Awareness Society.

SEPARATE THE MERIT FROM THE DRUNKARDS

196 Quote—letter to John Laurens, October 11, 1780, *PAH*.

197 Big thanks to Michael E. Newton for pointing out the enlisted promotion.

197 The list of merit and drunkards—from Allan McLane Hamilton's biography.

THINK SEVEN STEPS AHEAD

199 Quote—as reported in Allan McLane Hamilton's biography.

200 "cotton mills, a textile printing plant . . ."—Chernow.

200 Manufacturing quotes from "Report on the Subject of Manufactures," December 5, 1791.

202 Madison wanting to rent a navy from Portugal—via William Chrystal.

202 "Nation, despicable by its weakness"—*The Federalist* no. 11.

202 Adams insult—John Adams to *Boston Patriot*, May 29, 1809.

PRESERVE ORDER THROUGH PUNISHMENT

204 Quote, and the entirety of this entry: General Orders (to the army), January 4, 1800.

204 (Confession: I'm embarrassingly proud of this particular find.)

LEARN FROM YOUR ENEMIES

206 Quote—according to Thomas Jefferson in the *Anas*.

HIDE NOTHING

208 Quote—"Report Relative to the Loans Negotiated Under the Acts of the Fourth and Twelfth of August, 1790 [13–14 February 1793]," *PAH*.

208 ESPN-style Power Rankings, of course, are my own interpretation.

208 "His Holiness"—from the diary of Senator Maclay.

9. OFFICE POLITICS

PUBLISH OR PERISH

213 Quote—from "Fact No. 1," September 11, 1792, which really does, amazingly, end with "Fact." *PAH*.

215 Hamilton himself referenced the "cowardly assassin" barb in Catullus 1, 1792.

216 "Host within himself"—letter from Jefferson to Madison, September 21, 1795.

STAY ABOVE THE FRAY

218 Quote—via Joanne Freeman's *Affairs of Honor.*

219 Talleyrand quote—via Thomas Fleming.

219 The philosopher in question, of course, is Billy Joel.

220 "hissings, coughing, and hootings" via Freeman; she paints an evocative scene. (Check it out!)

220 "the necessity of a *full discussion*"—from contemporary newspaper, via Chernow.

220 "knock out Hamilton's brains"—from *The Life and Correspondence of Rufus King.*

SIDEBAR: HAMILTON: REPUBLICAN OR DEMOCRAT?

222 Krugman quote—from "In Hamilton's Debt," *New York Times,* April 22, 2016.

222 George Will quote—from his book *Restoration.* (And kudos to Will: he wrote those words in 1992, well before the bandwagon.)

LET OTHERS TAKE THE CREDIT

223 Quote, and anecdote—from Allan McLane Hamilton biography.

223 Basics here from Brookhiser.

JUMP AHEAD OF THE SCANDAL

226 The quote, of course, is from the Reynolds pamphlet.

226 . . . as is pretty much everything else here. Chernow and Brookhiser help us fill in the gaps.

232 The wine cooler letter—from Washington to Hamilton, August 21, 1797.

LET NO GOOD CRISIS GO TO WASTE

233 Quote—letter to Rufus King, February 6, 1799, *PAH.*

234 The Pickering/Adams conversations from John C. Hamilton's biography.

235 The Adams griping—letter to Oliver Wolcott, September 24, 1798, *PAH.*

235 "roofed with boards"—letter from Hamilton to James McHenry, October 3, 1799.

235 Burr/Hamilton conversation via Chernow.

235 "Squint at South America"—Hamilton to James McHenry, June 27, 1799, *PAH.*

238 West Point professor Jared Mansfield—letter to Jefferson January 21, 1821.

SIDEBAR: JOHN ADAMS'S SALTIEST INSULTS

239 Madison—letter to John Trumbull, April 25, 1790.

239 Franklin—letter to James Warren, April 13, 1783.

239 Jefferson—letter to Abigail Adams, December 26, 1793.

239 Washington—letter to Benjamin Rush, April 22, 1812. (In fairness, this quote is mostly about how, *despite* these limitations and deficiencies, Washington was effective.)

239 Aaron Burr—letter to Abigail Adams, November 18, 1794.

239 Franklin rebuttal—letter to Robert R. Livingston, July 1783.

NIP GOSSIP IN THE BUD

240 Quote—"David Gelston's Account of an Interview between Alexander Hamilton and James Monroe," July 11, 1797.

240 "we do not now live in the days of chivalry"—letter to William Gordon, September 5, 1779.

240 The Franklin quote and satire—an unpublished letter to Dr. Percival, July 17, 1784.

241 "The town is much agitated . . ."—once again from Senator Maclay, whose diary is a historical treasure trove. (Joanne Freeman discusses the importance of this journal at length in *Affairs of Honor.*)

DON'T. PRESS. SEND.

243 Quote—letter from Alexander Hamilton, "Concerning the Public Conduct and Character of John Adams, Esq., President of the United States," October 24, 1800.

243 Adams calling Hamilton an opium addict—letter to Benjamin Waterhouse, May 21, 1821.

246 Requesting friends for "new anecdotes"—letter to Timothy Pickering, November 13, 1800.

10. HONOR

NEVER BREAK A PROMISE (EVEN A TINY ONE)

249 Quote, and entire entry—letter to Philip, December 5, 1791, *PAH.*

TEACH A MORAL CODE

253 Quote—letter to Gouverneur Morris, February 29, 1802, *PAH.*

254 "Who do you call damned rascals?" quote via Chernow.

255 Thomas Fleming quote—here and elsewhere—via *Duel: Alexander Hamilton, Aaron Burr, and the Future of America.*

255 The 80 percent stat again courtesy of Fleming.

256 "On a bed without curtains" quote from his friend Henry Dawson, via Chernow.

SIDEBAR: WHAT IF BURR HAD MISSED?

258 As implied in the text, the entirety of this sidebar comes from the evil genius of Thomas Fleming.

ALWAYS FAITHFUL

259 Quote—via Chernow.

260 "Ancient philosophers"—letter to Eliza, November 19, 1798.

261 The gardening specifics from "Plan for a Garden, 1803," *PAH.*

261 Quotes from sons via Chernow.

CHARACTER FIRST

263 Quote—letter on September 26, 1792, *PAH.* (Recipient unknown.) Interesting that this letter was written more than a decade before the duel.

264 The "overworked fat man" morsel is from Fleming.

269 Chernow's wonderful research uncovered many of these newspaper quotes.

DEATH BEFORE DISHONOR

270 Quote—letter to Eliza, his final, on July 10, 1804, *PAH.*

279 Special thanks to Fleming here for many of the vivid dueling details.

HONOR YOUR COUNTRY

281 Quote—via Chernow.

281 Clarification—Hamilton said "take care of that pistol" *after* he was already in the boat.

282 "He was forty-seven years old." Assuming, of course, that you accept 1757 as Hamilton's birthday. If you're in the 1755 camp, he would have died at age 49.

283 Sedgwick's account of Burr's treasonous(?) aftermath is gripping.

285 "Single egg for dinner"—another gem from Sedgwick.

LEAVE A MARK

286 Quote—letter from Jefferson to Pierre-Samuel Du Pont de Nemours, January 18, 1802, *PAH*.

286 Somber NYC details courtesy of Stephen Knott.

286 The Morris eulogy connection via William Chrystal, whose *Hamilton by the Slice* is criminally overlooked.

289 Douglas Hamilton quotes—personal interview.

289 You're still reading? Really? Impressive. (You-know-who would approve.)

ADDITIONAL HAMILTON RESOURCES

—

THERE ARE GOBS AND gobs of amazing books on Hamilton. I hate to recommend just a few, as that does a disservice to the others, but, well, here are some that I found particularly useful:

Ron Chernow, *Alexander Hamilton*. There's a reason it sparked the idea for the musical.

Richard Brookhiser, *Alexander Hamilton, American*. Brookhiser's prose is a joy, and he somehow fits Hamilton's story into a cool 240 pages.

Joanne Freeman, *Affairs of Honor*. Her book covers more than just dueling—it gives a broader context for how honor is used as a currency and political tool.

Michael E. Newton, *Alexander Hamilton: The Formative Years*. Are you a fan of meticulous research? Then you're in for a treat. Newton spends 774 pages on *just the first part* of Hamilton's life; it's a tome of amazing facts.

Forrest McDonald, *Alexander Hamilton: A Biography*. Arguably the most philosophical of the biographies; digs into the intellectual undercurrents.

Stephen F. Knott, *Alexander Hamilton & The Persistence of Myth*. Just how is it that Hamilton faded from our collective memory? Knott gives us the answer.

Thomas Fleming, *Duel: Alexander Hamilton, Aaron Burr, and the Future of America*. Every page is gripping.

Founders.Archives.gov. A free collection of writings from the Founding Fathers—also includes Washington, Jefferson, Adams, and the gang. Fully searchable. It's delightful to read the Founders in their own words—without any interpretation or framing.

AllThingsHamilton.com—Website maintained by the Alexander Hamilton Awareness Society. Chock-full of Hamiltonian awesomeness.

Lin-Manuel Miranda and Jeremy McCarter, *Hamilton: The Revolution*. (Well, obvs.)

BIBLIOGRAPHY

The Adams Papers, Diary and Autobiography of John Adams, ed. L. H. Butterfield. Cambridge: Harvard University Press, 1961.

Brookhiser, Richard. *Alexander Hamilton, American*. New York: Touchstone, 1999.

Chrystal, William B. *Hamilton by the Slice: Falling in Love with Our Most Influential Founding Father*. Empire for Liberty, 2009.

Cohen, Stephen S., and J. Bradford Delong. *Concrete Economics: The Hamilton Approach to Economic Growth and Policy*. Harvard Business Review Press, 2016.

Chernow, Ron. *Alexander Hamilton*. New York: Penguin Press, 2004.

Ellis, Joseph J. *American Sphinx: The Character of Thomas Jefferson*. New York: Knopf, 1998.

Ellis, Joseph J. *The Quartet: Orchestrating the Second American Revolution, 1783–1789*. New York: Knopf, 2015.

Ferling, John. *John Adams: A Life*. New York: Oxford University Press, 1992.

Ferling, John. *Jefferson and Hamilton: The Rivalry That Forged a Nation*. New York: Bloomsbury Press, 2013.

Fleming, Thomas. *Duel: Alexander Hamilton, Aaron Burr and the Future of America*. New York: Basic Books, 1999.

Flexner, James Thomas. *The Young Hamilton: A Biography*. New York: Fordham University Press, 1997.

Ford, Henry Jones. *Alexander Hamilton*. Charles Scribner's Sons, 1925.

Freeman, Joanne B. *Affairs of Honor: National Politics in the New Republic*. New Haven: Yale University Press, 2001.

Hamilton, Alexander. *The Papers of Alexander Hamilton*. New York: Columbia University Press, 1961. (I made extensive use of the papers available online at Founders.Archive.gov. It's an excellent resource.)

Hamilton, Alexander, John Jay, and James Madison. *The Federalist Papers*. A Public Domain Book. Amazon Digital Services, n.d.

Hamilton, Allan McLane. *The Intimate Life of Alexander Hamilton*. London: Duckworth, 1910.

Hamilton, James A. *Reminiscences of James A. Hamilton; or, Men and*

Events, at Home and Abroad, during Three Quarters of a Century. New York. Scribner & Co., 1869.

Hamilton, John C. *The Life of Alexander Hamilton.* 2 vols. New York: D. Appleton, 1841.

Harper, John Lamberton. *American Machiavelli: Alexander Hamilton and the Origins of US Foreign Policy.* New York: Cambridge University Press, 2004.

Irving, Washington. *George Washington: A Biography.* New York: First Da Copa Press Edition, 1994.

Knott, Stephen F. *Alexander Hamilton and the Persistence of Myth.* Lawrence, Kansas: University Press of Kansas, 2002.

Knott, Stephen F., and Tony Williams. *Washington and Hamilton: The Alliance That Forged America.* Naperville, IL: Sourcebooks, 2015.

Lodge, Henry Cabot. *Alexander Hamilton.* Boston: Houghton Mifflin, 1884.

Maclay, William. *Journal of William Maclay.* Edited by Edgar S. Maclay. New York: D. Appleton, 1890.

McCullough, David. *John Adams.* New York: Simon & Schuster, 2001.

McDonald, Forrest. *Alexander Hamilton: A Biography.* New York: Norton, 1982.

Meacham, Jon. *Thomas Jefferson: The Art of Power.* New York: Random House, 2012.

Mitchell, Broadus. *Alexander Hamilton: A Concise Biography.* 1976. New York: Barnes & Noble, 2007.

Newton, Michael E. *Alexander Hamilton: The Formative Years.* Eleftheria Publishing, 2015.

Parton, James. *The Life and Times of Aaron Burr.* Boston and New York: Houghton Mifflin Company, originally 1857.

Randall, Willard Sterne. *Alexander Hamilton: A Life.* New York: HarperCollins, 2003.

Sedgwick, John. *War of Two: Alexander Hamilton, Aaron Burr, and the Duel that Stunned the Nation.* New York: Penguin Random House, 2015.

Sylla, Richard. "Financial Foundations: Public Credit, the National Bank, and Securities Markets." National Bureau of Economic Research, 2010.

Sylla, Richard. "Hamilton and the Federalist Financial Revolution, 1789–1795." *The New York Journal of American History,* 2004.

Will, George. *Restoration: Congress, Term Limits and the Recovery of Deliberative Democracy.* New York: The Free Press, 1992, www .columbia.edu/cu/philo/history/.

ABOUT THE AUTHOR

—

JEFF WILSER is the author of four prior books, including *The Maxims of Manhood* and *The Good News About What's Bad for You . . . and the Bad News About What's Good for You.* His work has appeared in print or online at *GQ, Esquire, New York* magazine, *Glamour, Cosmo, Bon Appétit, Condé Nast Traveler, Men's Fitness, mental floss, Comstock's,* and the *Huffington Post.* He lives in Brooklyn where, from his front door, he can see the site of a key battlefield in the Revolutionary War: In 1776, under heavy fire, Washington's army fled the British before linking up with a young artillery captain named Alexander Hamilton.

@JEFFWILSER